OFFICIAL SQA SPECIMEN QUESTION PAPER AND HODDER GIBSON MODEL QUESTION PAPERS WITH ANSWERS

NATIONAL 5

ENGLISH

2013 Specimen Question Paper & 2013 Model Papers

This book contains the official 2013 SQA Specimen Question Paper for National 5 English, with associated SQA approved answers modified from the official marking instructions that accompany the paper.

In addition the book contains model practice papers, together with answers, plus study skills advice. These papers, some of which may include a limited number of previously published SQA questions, have been specially commissioned by Hodder Gibson, and have been written by experienced senior teachers and examiners in line with the new National 5 syllabus and assessment outlines, Spring 2013. This is not SQA material but has been devised to provide further practice for National 5 examinations in 2014 and beyond.

Hodder Gibson is grateful to the copyright holders, as credited on the final page of the Answer Section, for permission to use their material. Every effort has been made to trace the copyright holders and to obtain their permission for the use of copyright material. Hodder Gibson will be happy to receive information allowing us to rectify any error or omission in future editions.

Hachette UK's policy is to use papers that are natural, renewable and recyclable products and made from wood grown in sustainable forests. The logging and manufacturing processes are expected to conform to the environmental regulations of the country of origin.

Orders: please contact Bookpoint Ltd, 130 Park Drive, Abingdon, Oxon OX14 4SE. Telephone: (44) 01235 827720. Fax: (44) 01235 400454. Lines are open 9.00–5.00, Monday to Saturday, with a 24-hour message answering service. Visit our website at www.hoddereducation.co.uk. Hodder Gibson can be contacted direct on: Tel: 0141 848 1609; Fax: 0141 889 6315; email: hoddergibson@hodder.co.uk

This collection first published in 2013 by
Hodder Gibson, an imprint of Hodder Education,
An Hachette UK Company
2a Christie Street
Paisley PA1 1NB

BrightRED   Hodder Gibson is grateful to Bright Red Publishing Ltd for collaborative work in preparation of this book and all SQA Past Paper
PUBLISHING   and National 5 Model Paper titles 2013.

Typeset by PDQ Digital Media Solutions Ltd, Bungay, Suffolk NR35 1BY

Printed in the UK

A catalogue record for this title is available from the British Library

ISBN: 978-1-4718-0207-2

3 2 1

2014 2013

Introduction

Study Skills – what you need to know to pass exams!

Pause for thought

Many students might skip quickly through a page like this. After all, we all know how to revise. Do you really though?

Think about this:

"IF YOU ALWAYS DO WHAT YOU ALWAYS DO, YOU WILL ALWAYS GET WHAT YOU HAVE ALWAYS GOT."

Do you like the grades you get? Do you want to do better? If you get full marks in your assessment, then that's great! Change nothing! This section is just to help you get that little bit better than you already are.

There are two main parts to the advice on offer here. The first part highlights fairly obvious things but which are also very important. The second part makes suggestions about revision that you might not have thought about but which WILL help you.

Part 1

DOH! It's so obvious but …

Start revising in good time

Don't leave it until the last minute – this will make you panic.

Make a revision timetable that sets out work time AND play time.

Sleep and eat!

Obvious really, and very helpful. Avoid arguments or stressful things too – even games that wind you up. You need to be fit, awake and focused!

Know your place!

Make sure you know exactly **WHEN and WHERE** your exams are.

Know your enemy!

Make sure you know what to expect in the exam.

How is the paper structured?

How much time is there for each question?

What types of question are involved?

Which topics seem to come up time and time again?

Which topics are your strongest and which are your weakest?

Are all topics compulsory or are there choices?

Learn by DOING!

There is no substitute for past papers and practice papers – they are simply essential! Tackling this collection of papers and answers is exactly the right thing to be doing as your exams approach.

Part 2

People learn in different ways. Some like low light, some bright. Some like early morning, some like evening / night. Some prefer warm, some prefer cold. But everyone uses their BRAIN and the brain works when it is active. Passive learning – sitting gazing at notes – is the most INEFFICIENT way to learn anything. Below you will find tips and ideas for making your revision more effective and maybe even more enjoyable. What follows gets your brain active, and active learning works!

Activity 1 – Stop and review

Step 1

When you have done no more than 5 minutes of revision reading STOP!

Step 2

Write a heading in your own words which sums up the topic you have been revising.

Step 3

Write a summary of what you have revised in no more than two sentences. Don't fool yourself by saying, 'I know it but I cannot put it into words'. That just means you don't know it well enough. If you cannot write your summary, revise that section again, knowing that you must write a summary at the end of it. Many of you will have notebooks full of blue/black ink writing. Many of the pages will not be especially attractive or memorable so try to liven them up a bit with colour as you are reviewing and rewriting. **This is a great memory aid, and memory is the most important thing.**

Activity 2 — Use technology!

Why should everything be written down? Have you thought about 'mental' maps, diagrams, cartoons and colour to help you learn? And rather than write down notes, why not record your revision material?

What about having a text message revision session with friends? Keep in touch with them to find out how and what they are revising and share ideas and questions.

Why not make a video diary where you tell the camera what you are doing, what you think you have learned and what you still have to do? No one has to see or hear it but the process of having to organise your thoughts in a formal way to explain something is a very important learning practice.

Be sure to make use of electronic files. You could begin to summarise your class notes. Your typing might be slow but it will get faster and the typed notes will be easier to read than the scribbles in your class notes. Try to add different fonts and colours to make your work stand out. You can easily Google relevant pictures, cartoons and diagrams which you can copy and paste to make your work more attractive and **MEMORABLE**.

Activity 3 – This is it. Do this and you will know lots!

Step 1

In this task you must be very honest with yourself! Find the SQA syllabus for your subject (www.sqa.org.uk). Look at how it is broken down into main topics called MANDATORY knowledge. That means stuff you MUST know.

Step 2

BEFORE you do ANY revision on this topic, write a list of everything that you already know about the subject. It might be quite a long list but you only need to write it once. It shows you all the information that is already in your long-term memory so you know what parts you do not need to revise!

Step 3

Pick a chapter or section from your book or revision notes. Choose a fairly large section or a whole chapter to get the most out of this activity.

With a buddy, use Skype, Facetime, Twitter or any other communication you have, to play the game "If this is the answer, what is the question?". For example, if you are revising Geography and the answer you provide is "meander", your buddy would have to make up a question like "What is the word that describes a feature of a river where it flows slowly and bends often from side to side?".

Make up 10 "answers" based on the content of the chapter or section you are using. Give this to your buddy to solve while you solve theirs.

Step 4

Construct a wordsearch of at least 10 X 10 squares. You can make it as big as you like but keep it realistic. Work together with a group of friends. Many apps allow you to make wordsearch puzzles online. The words and phrases can go in any direction and phrases can be split. Your puzzle must only contain facts linked to the topic you are revising. Your task is to find 10 bits of information to hide in your puzzle but you must not repeat information that you used in Step 3. DO NOT show where the words are. Fill up empty squares with random letters. Remember to keep a note of where your answers are hidden but do not show your friends. When you have a complete puzzle, exchange it with a friend to solve each other's puzzle.

Step 5

Now make up 10 questions (not "answers" this time) based on the same chapter used in the previous two tasks. Again, you must find NEW information that you have not yet used. Now it's getting hard to find that new information! Again, give your questions to a friend to answer.

Step 6

As you have been doing the puzzles, your brain has been actively searching for new information. Now write a NEW LIST that contains only the new information you have discovered when doing the puzzles. Your new list is the one to look at repeatedly for short bursts over the next few days. Try to remember more and more of it without looking at it. After a few days, you should be able to add words from your second list to your first list as you increase the information in your long-term memory.

FINALLY! Be inspired...

Make a list of different revision ideas and beside each one write **THINGS I HAVE** tried, **THINGS I WILL** try and **THINGS I MIGHT** try. Don't be scared of trying something new.

And remember – "FAIL TO PREPARE AND PREPARE TO FAIL!"

National 5 English

The course

The National 5 English course aims to enable you to develop the ability to:

- Listen, talk, read and write, as appropriate to purpose, audience and context
- Understand, analyse and evaluate texts, including Scottish texts, as appropriate to purpose and audience in the contexts of literature, language and media
- Create and produce texts, as appropriate to purpose, audience and context
- Apply knowledge and understanding of language.

How the course is graded

The grade you finally get for National 5 English depends on three things:

- The two internal Unit Assessments you do in school or college: "Analysis and Evaluation" and "Creation and Production"; these don't count towards the final grade, but you must have passed them before you can get a final grade
- Your Portfolio of Writing – this is submitted in April for marking by SQA and counts for 30% of your final grade
- The two exams you sit in May – that's what this book is all about.

The exams

Reading for Understanding, Analysis and Evaluation

- Exam time: 1 hour
- Total marks: 30
- Weighting in final grade: 30%
- What you have to do: read a passage and answer questions about it.

Critical Reading

- Exam time: 1 hour 30 minutes
- Total marks: 40
- Weighting in final grade: 40%
- What you have to do: Section A: write an essay about a work of literature you have studied during your course; Section B: read an extract from one of the Scottish Texts which are set for National 5 and answer questions about it.

Reading for Understanding, Analysis and Evaluation

Three important tips to start with

- Since there will always be a question asking you to summarise some or all of the passage, it is really important to read the whole passage before you even look at the questions. Doing this will give you a chance to get a rough idea of the main ideas in the passage, and you can add to this as you work your way through the questions.
- Pay close attention to the number of marks available for each question and make sure your answer is appropriate to the number of marks. In most questions, you will get 1 mark for each correct point.
- There is an instruction on the front cover of the exam paper to use "your own words as far as possible". This means you mustn't just copy chunks from the passage – you have to show that you understand what it means by rephrasing it in your own words.

Questions which ask for understanding

- Keep your answers fairly short and pay attention to the number of marks available.

Questions about language features

- This type of question will ask you to comment on features such as Word Choice, Imagery, Sentence Structure and Tone.
- You should pick out a relevant language feature and make a valid comment about its impact. Try to make your comments as specific as possible and avoid vague comments (like "It is a good word to use because it gives me a clear picture of what the writer is saying"). Some hints:

  - **Word Choice:** always try to pick a single word and then give its connotations, i.e. what it suggests

  - **Sentence Structure:** don't just name the feature – try to explain what effect it achieves **in that particular sentence**

  - **Imagery:** try to explain what the image means **literally** and then go on to explain what the writer is trying to say by using that image

- **Tone** this is always difficult – a good tip is to imagine the sentence or paragraph being read out loud and try to spot how the words or the structure give it a particular tone.

Summary questions

- Make sure you follow the instruction about what it is you are to summarise (the question will be as helpful as possible).
- Stick to the main ideas; avoid unimportant points and never include examples.
- Make sure you earn all the marks available for the question.

Critical Reading

Section 1 – Critical Essay

A common mistake is to rely too heavily on ideas and whole paragraphs you have used in practice essays and try to use them for the question you have chosen in the exam. The trick is to come to the exam with lots of ideas and thoughts about at least one of the texts you have studied and use these to tackle the question you choose from the exam paper. You mustn't use the exam question as an excuse to trot out an answer you've prepared in advance.

Structure

Every good essay has a structure, but there is no "correct" structure, no magic formula that the examiners are looking for. It's **your** essay, so structure it the way **you** want. As long as you're answering the question all the way through, then you'll be fine.

Relevance

Be relevant to the question **all the time** – not just in the first and last paragraphs.

Central Concerns

Try to make sure your essay shows that you have thought about and understood the central concerns of the text, i.e. what it's "about" – the ideas and themes the writer is exploring in the text.

Quotations

In poetry and drama essays, you're expected to quote from the text, but never fall into the trap of learning a handful of quotations and forcing them all into the essay regardless of the question you're answering. In prose essays, quotation is much less important, and you can show your knowledge more effectively by referring in detail to what happens in key sections of the novel or the short story.

Techniques

You are expected to show some understanding of how various literary techniques work within a text, but simply naming them will not get you marks, and structuring your essay around techniques rather than around relevant ideas in the text is not a good idea.

Section 2 – Scottish Text

The most important thing to remember here is that there are two very different types of question to be answered:

- Three or four questions (for a total of 12 marks) which focus entirely on the extract
- One question (for 8 marks) which requires knowledge of the whole text (or of another poem or short story by the same writer).

The first type of question will often ask you to use the same type of close textual analysis skills you used in the Reading part of your Analysis and Evaluation Unit. There can also be a question asking for the type of summary skills you're used to in the Reading part of the exam. The golden rule is to read each question very carefully and do exactly as instructed.

The second type of question is really the same as a Critical Essay. Obviously, for 8 marks you're not expected to write as much as you are in a 20-mark essay, but your approach should be pretty much the same, and you should write as much as you can – as long as it's relevant to the question.

Final bit of advice for the Scottish Text question: when you see the extract in the exam paper, don't get too confident just because you recognise it (you certainly should recognise it if you've studied properly!) And even if you've answered questions on it before, remember that the questions in the exam are likely to be different, so stay alert.

Good luck!

Remember that the rewards for passing National 5 English are well worth it! Your pass will help you get the future you want for yourself. In the exam, be confident in your own ability. If you're not sure how to answer a question, trust your instincts and just give it a go anyway – keep calm and don't panic! GOOD LUCK!

2013 Specimen Question Paper

National
Qualifications
SPECIMEN ONLY

SQ13/N5/01

**English
Reading for Understanding,
Analysis and Evaluation**

Date — Not applicable

Duration — 1 hour

Total marks — 30

When you are told to do so, open the booklet, read the passage and attempt all the questions, using your own words as far as possible.

Before attempting the questions you must check that your answer booklet is for the same subject and level as this question paper.

On the answer booklet, you must clearly identify the question number you are attempting.

Use **blue** or **black** ink.

Before leaving the examination room you must give your answer booklet to the Invigilator. If you do not, you may lose all the marks for this paper.

The following article is about JK Rowling (the creator of Harry Potter) and the nature of fame.

Fame conveys the illusion of intimacy. We assume we know everything there is to know about the person concerned, from David Beckham's wardrobe to Prince William's childhood nicknames. The story of JK Rowling writing in a café with a prolonged cup of coffee to avoid a cold flat is almost as familiar as she is.

5   So it comes as a shock when an individual tone of voice penetrates those layers of gossip and assumption. The voices may not be quite what we imagined. Beckham, mythologised for his looks and skill, sounds insufficiently heroic when he speaks. A rare television interview with JK Rowling, broadcast this week, to mark the publication of *Harry Potter and the Order of the Phoenix*, revealed a thoroughly modern woman who speaks, not in

10   the modulated tones that might be expected of a children's classic author, but just like the rest of us.

Even the sound of Prince William chatting with his father and brother in a 21st birthday video is a surprise, after years when, like his mother, his image was familiar but his voice was rarely heard.

15   Rowling is loved for her stories, but also for her story. A contemporary Cinderella, she endured the cold flat and life on single-parent benefit. Then Harry happened and she went to the ball. Neil Murray, her husband, might be abashed to find himself cast as Prince Charming, but her life has changed as much as any scullery-maid turned princess.

The missing part of the Cinderella story is what happens when she puts on the glass

20   slipper and disappears into the palace. Rowling filled in the blanks, describing to Jeremy Paxman how she has to cope with begging letters, journalists rifling through her bins, photographers lurking on the beach, and strangers accosting her in the supermarket.

The writer was honest enough to admit that the massive success of Harry Potter had given her a sense of validation. "I don't feel like quite such a waste of space anymore." Like

25   David Beckham, taking care to thank Manchester United fans as his transfer to Real Madrid was announced, she is keenly aware of the true source of her popularity, guarding plots and characters in the interests of children who would be sad to have the story spoilt.

But Rowling was also frank about unexpected aspects of her fame. She feels guilty about

30   her wealth – denying she is worth the rumoured 280 million – and fears life after Harry, citing AA Milne, who could never get a book reviewed without Pooh and Tigger being mentioned.

Fame, as she implied, freezes you in one frame. Prince William will be lucky ever to take refuge in a proper job. David Beckham will always mean football, and Rowling, who

35   disclosed that she has tried her hand at a novel for adults, will have to write very brilliantly to discard the label of a children's writer.

Beckham exploits to his advantage the way in which the famous are transformed into products often with scant relation to their actual lives or personalities. He treats himself as a logo. In the week that his transfer was announced, he was touring Japan with his

40   wife, endorsing products.

This is a facet of celebrity that Rowling detests, describing the task of agreeing Potter merchandise as "horrible". But writers, unlike footballers, need not fear an early sell-by date for their skills.

45 William, of course, has nothing to sell – or has he? His face, youth and ease are guarantees that the monarchy can adapt and move into the 21st century. The palace both protects and carefully markets him, controlling access and exposure. Is he willing to surrender the chance of a relatively normal life to be the modern face of monarchy? For him, as for Rowling, the debate about a possible privacy law, kick-started this week by a committee of MPs, has intense personal relevance.

50 William at least has the consolation that his fame derives from his parentage, not from himself. Unless Britain turns republic, he will always be royal. But for those whose fame is built on personality, one crack brings the edifice crashing down.

JK Rowling is fortunate in that the reason for her fame exists at one remove from her. Harry is nothing to do with who her parents were, or how good she looks on television.
55 He is the product of her imagination, interacting with the imagination of millions of others. Just as the books, with their literary allusions and cultural quirks, borrow from other traditions, so the wizard world is held in common. Internet sites discuss the plot, translators try to render "Hogwarts" in other languages. Harry is public property in a way that his creator, despite the dustbins and long lenses, is not.

60 In an age of appearances, her story should reassure us. JK Rowling found success and made millions through trusting her own invention. We will never know her, but we know Harry, and his magic is likely to last.

Adapted from an article in the The Scotsman newspaper, June 2003.

MARKS

1. "Fame conveys the illusion of intimacy." **In your own words**, explain how examples the writer gives in the first paragraph illustrate this idea.

3

2. Look at lines 15–18. **In your own words**, explain what comparisons the writer draws between JK Rowling and Cinderella.

4

3. Explain how the writer's word choice in lines 19–22 helps to show the negative effects of fame.

4

4. For JK Rowling, what are the advantages and disadvantages of fame? Refer to lines 23–36 in your answer, **using your own words**.

4

5. Choose **one** of the two rhetorical questions in paragraph 11 (lines 44–49) and discuss its effect.

2

6. **In your own words**, explain fully in what ways JK Rowling feels she is "fortunate" (line 53). Give evidence from lines 53–62 to support your answer.

4

7. Read the last paragraph. Identify the writer's attitude to JK Rowling in this paragraph and give evidence to support your answer.

2

8. Choose **one** of the following images:

"Fame, as she implied, freezes you in one frame." (line 33)

"He treats himself as a logo." (lines 38–39)

"But for those whose fame is built on personality, one crack brings the edifice crashing down." (lines 51–52)

Explain what your chosen image means and analyse its effect.

3

9. Referring to the whole article, **in your own words** list the key points the writer makes about the nature of fame.

4

[END OF SPECIMEN QUESTION PAPER]

Acknowledgement of Copyright

Extract is adapted from an article titled "Reassuring message of Rowling's wizard world" taken from The Scotsman. Permission sought from Johnston Press plc.

National
Qualifications
SPECIMEN ONLY

SQ13/N5/02

English
Critical Reading

Date — Not applicable

Duration — 1 hour and 30 minutes

Total marks — 40

SECTION 1 — 20 marks

Write ONE critical essay on a previously studied text from Drama, Prose, Poetry, Film and TV Drama or Language Study.

SECTION 2 — 20 marks

Read an extract from a Scottish text you have previously studied and attempt the questions.

You should spend approximately 45 minutes on each section.

Before attempting the questions you must check that your answer booklet is for the same subject and level as this question paper.

On the answer booklet, you must clearly identify the question number you are attempting.

Use **blue** or **black** ink.

Before leaving the examination room you must give your answer booklet to the Invigilator. If you do not, you may lose all the marks for this paper.

SECTION 1 — CRITICAL ESSAY — 20 marks

Attempt ONE question from this section of the paper from ONE of the Parts A–E.

You may use a Scottish text but <u>not</u> the one used in Section 2.

Your essay should be on a different <u>genre</u> to the one used in Section 2.

Write the number of your chosen question in the margin of your answer.

You should spend about 45 minutes on the essay.

PART A — DRAMA

> *Answers to questions in this part should refer to the text and to such relevant features as characterisation, key scene(s), structure, climax, theme, plot, conflict, setting . . .*

1. Choose a play which you feel has a turning-point.

    Describe briefly what happens at this turning point and then, by referring to appropriate techniques, go on to explain how it makes an impact on the play as a whole.

2. Choose a play in which the playwright presents a flawed character who you feel is more worthy of our sympathy than criticism.

    By referring to appropriate techniques, show how the character's flawed nature is revealed, then explain how, despite this, we are led to feel sympathy for her/him.

PART B — PROSE

> *Answers to questions in this part should refer to the text and to such relevant features as characterisation, setting, language, key incident(s), climax, turning point, plot, structure, narrative technique, theme, ideas, description . . .*

3. Choose a novel **or** a short story **or** a work of non-fiction which explores an important theme.

    By referring to appropriate techniques, show how the author has explored this theme.

4. Choose a novel **or** a short story in which the author creates a fascinating character.

    By referring to appropriate techniques, show how the author has created this character and why you found him/her so fascinating.

PART C — POETRY

> *Answers to questions in this part should refer to the text and to such relevant features as word choice, tone, imagery, structure, content, rhythm, rhyme, theme, sound, ideas . . .*

5. Choose a poem which made a lasting impression on you.

   Explain briefly what the poem is about, then, by referring to appropriate techniques, show how the poem has made this lasting impression.

6. Choose a poem which features an encounter or an incident.

   By referring to appropriate techniques, show how the poet's development of the encounter or incident leads you to a deeper understanding of the poem's central concerns.

PART D — FILM AND TV DRAMA

> *Answers to questions in this part should refer to the text and to such relevant features as use of camera, key sequence, characterisation, mise-en-scène, editing, setting, music/sound, special effects, plot, dialogue . . .*

7. Choose a scene or sequence from a film **or** TV drama* which had an impact on you.

   Briefly describe the events which led to this scene or sequence, then, by referring to appropriate techniques, go on to show how this impact was created.

8. Choose a film or TV drama* which belongs to a particular genre (e.g. crime, adventure, romance, soap opera, sit-com, thriller...).

   By referring to appropriate techniques, explain how the film or television makers have used features of this genre effectively.

* "TV drama" includes a single play, a series or a serial.

PART E — LANGUAGE STUDY

Answers to questions in this part should refer to the text and to such relevant features as register, accent, dialect, slang, jargon, vocabulary, tone, abbreviation . . .

9. Choose a print or non-print text which aims to persuade people.

   By referring to specific examples from your chosen text, show how persuasive techniques are used to engage the reader/viewer.

10. Consider a form of communication used by a particular group of people.

    By referring to appropriate techniques such as distinctive vocabulary or grammatical constructions, show how the group's language is different from that used by the general population and discuss the advantages to the group of using its specific language.

SECTION 2 — SCOTTISH TEXT — 20 marks

Attempt only ONE question from ONE of the three parts (Drama, Prose or Poetry).
You must choose a different genre to the text you used in Section 1.

You should spend about 45 minutes on this question.

Read the extract carefully and then attempt ALL the questions below the extract,
<u>using your own words as far as possible</u>.

SCOTTISH TEXT (DRAMA)

Read the extract below and then attempt the following questions.

Question 1

The Steamie by Tony Roper

(*Magrit's Monologue*)

MAGRIT: (*this speech should be done with heavy irony to the audience*)

Isn't it wonderful tae be a woman. Ye get up at the crack o' dawn and get the breakfast oan, get the weans ready and oot the hoose lookin' as tidy and as well dressed as ye can afford. Then ye see tae the lord high provider and get him oot, then wash up, finish the ironin', tidy the hoose and gie the flair a skite o'er. Then it's oot tae yer ain wee job, mebbe cleanin' offices, servin' in a shop or washin' stairs. Then it's dinner time. Well it is fur everybody else but no us 'cause we don't get dinner. By the time yer oot and run home, cooked something for the weans yer lucky if you feel like something tae eat. I know I don't and even if I did . . . the dinner hour's finished, so it's back tae yer work; that is efter ye've goat in whatever yer gonna gie them for their tea, and efter yer finished yer work, ye'r back up . . . cookin' again and they'll tell ye the mince is lumpy . . . or the chips are too warm . . . then they're away oot. The weans tae play . . . the men tae have a drink, cause they need wan . . . the souls . . . efter pittin' in a hard day's graft, so ye've goat the hoose tae yersel' and what dae ye dae, ye tidy up again don't ye? Mer ironin, light the fire, wash the dishes and the pots etc, etc. and then ye sit doon. And what happens . . . ye've just sat doon when the weans come up. 'Gonnae make us a cuppa tea and something tae eat' . . . What dae ye's want tae eat? . . . 'Och anything Ma' . . . D'ye want some o' that soup? . . . 'Naw' . . . A tomato sandwich? . . . 'Naw' . . . A couple o' boiled eggs? . . . 'Naw' . . . A piece 'n spam? . . . 'Naw' . . . Well what d'ye's want? . . . 'Och anything at all'. So ye make them something tae eat then ye sit doon and finally have a wee blaw . . . a very wee blaw . . . cause it's time tae go tae the steamie. Ye go tae the steamie, finish at nine o'clock and get the washin' hame. Ye sort it aw oot . . . and get it put by and then sometimes mebbe take stock of yer life. What are we? . . . skivvies . . . unpaid skivvies . . . in other words we are . . . used . . . but ye think tae yersel', well even if I am being used . . . I don't mind . . . cause I love my family and anyway it's New Year's Eve. I can relax and jist enjoy masel . . . and any minute noo the weans'll be in an ma friends'll be comin' roon wi' black bun, shortbread, dumplin's, a wee refreshment and I can forget aw ma worries even if it's jist for a night and the weans arrive and ye gie them shortbread, sultana cake, ginger wine and there is just one thing missin', the head of the family. The door bell goes, ye open the door, and what is staunin there, ready to make the evening complete . . . that's right . . . your husband, your better half . . . the man who was goin' to make you the happiest woman in the world and (*Gently.*) what does he look like . . . *that.* (*At* ANDY.)

MARKS

Question 1 (continued)

Questions

1. In your own words, summarise the ways in which women's lives at the time could be seen to be difficult. Make at least four key points.   **4**

2. Magrit feels that women's efforts are not appreciated. Show how this is revealed through word choice.   **2**

3. With close reference to the text, explain how the playwright reveals Magrit's feelings towards:

    (a) her children;   **3**

    (b) her husband.   **3**

4. Gender is an important theme in this extract. With close reference to the rest of the play, explain how the theme of gender is explored.   **8**

OR

SCOTTISH TEXT (PROSE)

Read the extract below and then attempt the following questions.

Question 2

Treasure Island **by Robert Louis Stevenson**

In this extract, which is from Chapter 3 of the book, the narrator, Jim Hawkins, gives an account of the visit to the Admiral Benbow Inn of the pirate Blind Pew.

So things passed until, the day after the funeral, and about three o'clock of a bitter, foggy, frosty afternoon, I was standing at the door for a moment, full of sad thoughts about my father, when I saw someone drawing slowly near along the road. He was plainly blind, for he tapped before him with a stick, and wore a great green shade over his eyes
5   and nose; and he was hunched, as if with age or weakness, and wore a huge old tattered seacloak with a hood, that made him appear positively deformed. I never saw in my life a more dreadful looking figure. He stopped a little from the inn, and, raising his voice in an odd sing-song, addressed the air in front of him:-

"Will any kind friend inform a poor blind man, who has lost the precious sight of his eyes
10   in the gracious defence of his native country, England, and God bless King George! Where or in what part of this country he may now be?"

"You are at the 'Admiral Benbow', Black Hill Cove, my good man," said I.

"I hear a voice," said he - "a young voice. Will you give me your hand, my kind young friend, and lead me in?"

15   I held out my hand, and the horrible, soft-spoken, eyeless creature gripped it in a moment like a vice. I was so much startled that I struggled to withdraw; but the blind man pulled me close up to him with a single action of his arm.

"Now boy," he said, "take me to the captain."

"Sir," said I, "upon my word I dare not."

20   "Oh," he sneered, "that's it! Take me in straight, or I'll break your arm."

And he gave it, as he spoke, a wrench that made me cry out.

"Sir," I said, "it is for yourself I mean. The captain is not what he used to be. He sits with a drawn cutlass. Another gentleman —"

"Come, now march," interrupted he; and I never heard a voice so cruel, and cold, and
25   ugly as that blind man's. It cowed me more than the pain; and I began to obey him at once, walking straight in at the door and towards the parlour where our sick old buccaneer was sitting, dazed with rum. The blind man clung close to me, holding me in one iron fist, and leaning almost more of his weight on me than I could carry. "Lead me straight up to him, and when I'm in view, cry out, 'Here's a friend for you Bill.' If you
30   don't, I'll do this," and with that he gave me a twitch that I thought would have made me faint. Between this and that, I was so utterly terrified of the blind beggar that I forgot my terror of the captain, and as I opened the parlour door, cried out the words he had ordered in a trembling voice.

The poor captain raised his eyes, and at one look the rum went out of him, and left him
35   staring sober. The expression of his face was not so much of terror as of mortal sickness. He made a movement to rise, but I do not believe he had enough force left in his body.

Question 2 (continued)

"Now, Bill, sit where you are," said the beggar. "If I can't see, I can hear a finger stirring. Business is business. Hold out your right hand. Boy, take his right hand by the wrist, and bring it near to my right."

40 We both obeyed him to the letter, and I saw him pass something from the hollow of the hand that held his stick into the palm of the captain's, which closed upon it instantly.

"And now that's done," said the blind man; and at the words he suddenly left hold of me, and with incredible accuracy and nimbleness, skipped out of the parlour and into the road, where, as I still stood motionless, I could hear his stick go tap-tap-tapping into the
45 distance.

It was some time before either I or the captain seemed to gather our senses; but at length, and about the same moment, I released his wrist, which I was still holding, and he drew in his hand and looked sharply into the palm.

"Ten o'clock!" he cried. "Six hours. We'll do them yet!" and he sprang to his feet.

50 Even as he did so, he reeled, put his hand to his throat, stood swaying for a moment, and then, with a peculiar sound, fell from his whole height face foremost to the floor.

I ran to him at once, calling to my mother. But haste was all in vain. The captain had been struck by thundering apoplexy. It was a curious thing to understand for I had certainly never liked the man, though of late I had begun to pity him, but as soon as I saw
55 that he was dead, I burst into a flood of tears. It was the second death I had known, and the sorrow of the first was still fresh in my heart.

Questions

1. Summarise what happens in this extract from the novel. Make at least **three** key points.   3

2. Look at paragraph 1 (lines 1–8).

    What is the mood or atmosphere created by the writer, and how does the writer use language effectively to create this mood or atmosphere?   3

3. Look again at lines 9–27 ("Will any kind friend...dazed with rum.")

    Show how any **two** examples of the writer's use of language contribute to a growing sense of menace.   4

4. Look at line 46 ("It was some time before either I or the captain seemed to gather our senses.") From the "beggar's" behaviour up to this point, what is it that has so surprised them?   2

5. By referring to this extract, and to at least **two** other incidents from elsewhere in the novel, explain how the character of Jim changes and develops as the story progresses.   8

OR

SCOTTISH TEXT (POETRY)

Read the poem below and then attempt the following questions.

Question 3

Song Composed in August by Robert Burns

Now westlin winds and slaught'ring guns
Bring Autumn's pleasant weather;
And the moorcock springs on whirring wings
Amang the blooming heather:
Now waving grain, wide o'er the plain,
Delights the weary farmer;
And the moon shines bright, when I rove at night,
To muse upon my charmer.

The partridge loves the fruitful fells,
The plover loves the mountains;
The woodcock haunts the lonely dells,
The soaring hern the fountains:
Thro' lofty groves the cushat roves,
The path of man to shun it;
The hazel bush o'erhangs the thrush
The spreading thorn the linnet.

Thus ev'ry kind their pleasure find,
The savage and the tender;
Some social join, and leagues combine,
Some solitary wander:
Avaunt away! the cruel sway
Tyrannic man's dominion;
The sportsman's joy, the murd'ring cry,
The flutt'ring, gory pinion!

But Peggy dear, the ev'ning's clear,
Thick flies the skimming swallow,
The sky is blue, the fields in view,
All fading-green and yellow:
Come let us stray our gladsome way,
And view the charms of Nature;
The rustling corn, the fruited thorn,
And ev'ry happy creature.

We'll gently walk, and sweetly talk,
Till the silent moon shine clearly;
I'll grasp thy waist, and, fondly prest,
Swear how I love thee dearly:
Not vernal show'rs to budding flow'rs,
Now Autumn to the farmer,
So dear can be as thou to me,
My fair, my lovely charmer.

Question 3 (continued)

Questions

1. Many of the main ideas or concerns of the poem come across clearly in the first stanza.

   (a) Identify **two** of these main ideas or concerns from stanza one.   **2**

   (b) Show how **two** examples of the poet's use of language in stanza one help to clarify or illustrate his meaning.   **4**

2. Show how any **two** examples of the poet's use of language in stanza two or stanza three effectively contribute to the main ideas or concerns of the poem.   **4**

3. How effective do you find any aspect of the final two stanzas as a conclusion to the poem?

   Your answer might deal with ideas and and/or language.   **2**

4. With close textual reference, show how the ideas and/or language of this poem are similar **OR** different to another poem or poems by Burns which you have read.   **8**

[END OF SPECIMEN QUESTION PAPER]

Acknowledgement of Copyright

Extract is taken from "The Steamie" in "Scot-free: New Scottish Plays", Play by Tony Roper and "Scot-free" by Alasdair Cameron (ed). Reproduced by permission of Nick Hern Books Ltd.

NATIONAL 5

2013 Model Paper 1

N5

National
Qualifications
MODEL PAPER 1

English
Reading for Understanding,
Analysis and Evaluation

Duration — 1 hour

Total marks — 30

When you are told to do so, open the booklet, read the passage and attempt all the questions, using your own words as far as possible.

HODDER
GIBSON
LEARN MORE

SUPERSTITION

In this passage, the writer explores how superstition can both help and hinder us.

Tennis players are a funny bunch. Have you noticed how they always ask for three balls instead of two; how they bounce the ball the same number of times before serving, as if any deviation from their routine might bring the world collapsing on their heads?

But the superstitions and rituals so beloved by the world's top players are not confined to the
5   court. They take even more bizarre twists when the poor dears get home after their matches. Goran Ivanisevic got it into his head that if he won a match he had to repeat everything he did the previous day, such as eating the same food at the same restaurant, talking to the same people and watching the same TV programmes. One year this meant that he had to watch Teletubbies every morning during his Wimbledon campaign. "Sometimes it got very boring," he
10 said.

Could it be that these multifarious superstitions tell us something of deeper importance not only about humanity but about other species on the planet?

The answer, I think, is to be found in the world of pigeon. Yes, really. These feathered fellows, you see, are the tennis players of the bird world. Don't take my word for it: that was the
15 opinion of B. F. Skinner, the man widely regarded as the father of modern psychology.

Skinner's view was based on a groundbreaking experiment that he carried out in 1947 in which he placed some hungry pigeons in a cage attached to an automatic mechanism that delivered food "at regular intervals with no reference whatsoever to the bird's behaviour". He discovered that the pigeons associated the delivery of the food with whatever chance actions they happened to be
20 performing at the moment it was first delivered. So what did the pigeons do? They kept performing the same actions, even though they had no effect whatsoever on the release of food.

I know, I know. This is nothing compared with the weird behaviour that goes on at Wimbledon, but do you see the connection? The pigeons were acting as if they could influence the mechanism delivering the Trill in just the same way that Ivanisevic thought that he could
25 influence the outcome of his next match by watching Teletubbies. To put it a tad formally, they both witnessed a random connection between a particular kind of behaviour and a desired outcome, and then (wrongly) inferred that one causedthe other.

Superstitious behaviour emerged quite early in evolutionary history. What is certain is that it is widespread, particularly within *homo sapiens*. More than half of Americans admitted to being
30 superstitious in a recent poll, and it is not just silly and gullible types either. At Harvard University, students frequently rub the foot of the statue of John Harvard for good luck.

Even cricketers, perhaps the brightest and most sensible sportsmen of all (well, that's what they tell us), are not immune to superstition. Jack Russell, the former England wicketkeeper, was among the most notorious, refusing to change his hat or wicketkeeping pads throughout his
35 career, even though they became threadbare and smelly, something that really got up the noses of his team-mates.

But this raises another, deeper question: why do so many of us maintain rituals of various kinds when they have no real connection with the desired outcome? Or, to put it another way, why is superstitious behaviour so widespread, not just within our species but beyond, when it seems to
40 confer no tangible benefits? It's here that things get really interesting (and just a little complex). And, as with most interesting things, the answeris to be found in deep evolutionary history.

Imagine a caveman going to pick some berries from some bushes near his rocky abode. He hears some rustling in the bushes and wrongly infers that there is a lion lurking in there and scarpers.
45 He even gets a little superstitious about those bushes and gives them a wide berth in future. Is this superstition a problem to our caveman? Well, not if there are plenty other berry-bearing bushes from which to get his five-a-day.

But suppose that there really is a lion living in those bushes. The caveman's behaviour now looks not only sensible but life-saving. So, a tendency to perceive connections that do not actually
50 exist can confer huge evolutionary benefits, providing a cocoon of safety in a turbulent and dangerous world.   The only proviso (according to some devilishly complicated mathematics known as game theory) is this: your superstitions must not impose too much of a burden on those occasions when they are without foundation.

And this is almost precisely what superstitions look like in the modern world. Some believe in
55 horoscopes, but few allow them to dictate their behaviour; some like to wear the same lucky shoes to every job interview, but it is not as if wearing a different pair would improve their chances of success; some like to bounce the ball precisely seven times before serving at tennis, but although they are wrong to suppose that this ball-bouncing is implicated in their success, it does not harm their prospects.

60 It is only when a superstition begins to compromise our deeper goals and aspirations that we have moved along the spectrum of irrationality far enough to risk a diagnosis of obsessive compulsive disorder. Take Kolo Touré, the former Arsenal defender who insists on being the last player to leave the dressing room after the half-time break. No real problem, you might think, except that when William Gallas, his team-mate, was injured and needed treatment at half-time
65 during a match, Touré stayed in the dressing room until Gallas had been treated, forcing Arsenal to start the second half with only nine players.

When a superstition that is supposed to help you actually hinders you, it is probably time to kick the ritual into touch. With a rabbit's foot, obviously.

Adapted from an article by Matthew Syed in The Times.

MARKS

Questions

1. In line 14, the writer says that pigeons "are the tennis players of the bird world". Referring to key ideas in lines 1-27, explain what he means by this. **4**

2. Read lines 28-36.

   (a) What impression does the writer create of Goran Ivanisevic in these lines? **2**

   (b) How does the writer convey surprise at the behaviour of Jack Russell? **2**

3. Explain **in your own words** what key points the writer is illustrating by referring to the caveman (lines 43-53). **4**

4. Describe the key features of the **sentence structure** in lines 54-59 and explain how it helps to convey the writer's main point. **4**

5. Read lines 60-63.

   (a) Explain how effective you find the word "spectrum" (line 61) as an **image** or **metaphor** to illustrate people's "irrationality". **2**

   (b) Why does the writer include the anecdote about the footballer Kolo Touré (lines 62-66)? **2**

   (c) How effective do you find the tone of the last paragraph (lines 67-68) as a conclusion to the passage? **2**

6. A common feature of the writer's style in this passage is to use words or expressions which are unexpected in order to create a light-hearted tone. Find **two** examples of this from lines 1-47 and explain what is unexpected about each. **4**

7. Referring to the whole article, list **in your own words** the key points the writer makes about superstitions. **4**

[END OF PRACTICE QUESTION PAPER]

National Qualifications
MODEL PAPER 1

English
Critical Reading

Duration — 1 hour and 30 minutes

Total marks — 40

SECTION 1 — 20 marks

Write ONE critical essay on a previously studied text from Drama, Prose, Poetry, Film and TV Drama or Language Study.

SECTION 2 — 20 marks

Read an extract from a Scottish text you have previously studied and attempt the questions.

You should spend approximately 45 minutes on each section.

HODDER
GIBSON
LEARN MORE

SECTION 1 — CRITICAL ESSAY — 20 marks

Attempt ONE question from this section of the paper from ONE of the Parts A-E.

You may use a Scottish text but <u>not</u> the one used in Section 2.

Your essay should be on a different <u>genre</u> to the one used in Section 2.

Write the number of your chosen question in the margin of your answer.

You should spend about 45 minutes on the essay.

PART A — DRAMA

Answers to questions in this part should refer to the text and to such relevant features as characterisation, key scene(s), structure, climax, theme, plot, conflict, setting . . .

1. Choose a play in which there is conflict between two characters in a family **or** a group.

   Show how the conflict occurs and then, by referring to appropriate techniques, explain how it affects the characters and the events of the play.

2. Choose a play in which a main character's actions have a significant effect on the rest of the play.

   By referring to appropriate techniques, show how this character's actions have affected the other characters **and/or** the outcome of the play.

PART B — PROSE

Answers to questions in this part should refer to the text and to such relevant features as characterisation, setting, language, key incident(s), climax, turning point, plot, structure, narrative technique, theme, ideas, description . . .

3. Choose a novel **or** short story in which you feel sympathy with one of the main characters because of the difficulties or injustice or hardships she or he has to face.

   Describe the problems the character faces and, by referring to appropriate techniques, show how you are made to feel sympathy for her or him.

4. Choose a novel **or** a short story **or** a work of non-fiction in which the writer uses a memorable style/voice/narrative technique.

   By referring to appropriate techniques, explain in detail how features of the writing style/voice/narrative technique contribute to the effectiveness of the text.

PART C — POETRY

Answers to questions in this part should refer to the text and to such relevant features as word choice, tone, imagery, structure, content, rhythm, rhyme, theme, sound, ideas . . .

5. Choose a poem which describes a person's experience.

   By referring to appropriate techniques, explain how the description of the experience makes the poem more interesting.

6. Choose a poem which has as one of its central concerns a personal, social or religious issue.

   By referring to appropriate techniques, show how the poem increases your understanding of the issue.

PART D — FILM AND TV DRAMA

Answers to questions in this part should refer to the text and to such relevant features as use of camera, key sequence, characterisation, mise-en-scène, editing, setting, music/ sound, special effects, plot, dialogue . . .

7. Choose a film or TV drama* which has a character who could be described as a hero or as a villain.

   By referring to appropriate techniques, explain how the character is introduced and then developed throughout the film or TV drama.

8. Choose a sequence from a film which is important both to the atmosphere and to the plot of the film.

   By referring to appropriate techniques, show how atmosphere is created in the sequence and go on to show how the sequence and the atmosphere are important to the film as a whole.

* "TV drama" includes a single play, a series or a serial.

PART E — LANGUAGE STUDY

Answers to questions in this part should refer to the text and to such relevant features as register, accent, dialect, slang, jargon, vocabulary, tone, abbreviation . . .

9. Consider the differences between written language and an aspect of spoken language which you have studied.

   By referring to specific examples and to appropriate features of language, explain the similarities and differences between the two forms of language you have studied.

10. Consider the language of advertising.

   In any one advertisement identify the ways in which language is used successfully. By referring to specific examples and to appropriate features of language, explain what it is about these usages which make them effective.

SECTION 2 — SCOTTISH TEXT — 20 marks

Attempt only ONE question from ONE of the three parts (Drama, Prose or Poetry).

You must choose a different genre to the text you used in Section 1.

You should spend about 45 minutes on this question.

Read the extract carefully and then attempt ALL the questions below the extract, using your own words as far as possible.

SCOTTISH TEXT (DRAMA)

Read the extract below and then attempt the following questions.

Question 1

Sailmaker by Alan Spence

This extract is from Act One of the play.

> (*Enter DAVIE and BILLY, talking as they walk*)

DAVIE: Eh, Billy ... that coupla quid ah tapped off ye. Could it wait till next week?

 BILLY: Aye sure.

DAVIE: Things are still a wee bit tight.

5   BILLY: What's the score?

DAVIE: Eh?

 BILLY: Ye shouldnae be this skint. What is it?

DAVIE: Ah told ye. It's the job. Just hasnae been so great. No sellin enough. No collectin enough. No getting much over the basic.

10   BILLY: Aye, but ye should be able tae get by. Just the two ae ye.

DAVIE: It's no easy.

 BILLY: Ye bevvyin?

DAVIE: Just a wee half when ah finish ma work. An by Christ ah need it.

15   BILLY: Ye bettin too heavy? Is that it?

DAVIE: (*Hesitates then decides to tell him*) It started a coupla months ago. Backed a favourite. Absolutely surefire certainty. Couldnae lose. But it was even money, so ah had tae put quite a whack on it. (*Slightly shamefaced*) Best part ae a week's wages.

20   BILLY: An it got beat?

DAVIE: Out the park. So ah made it up by borrowin off the bookie. He does his moneylender on the side. Charges interest.

BILLY: An every week ye miss the interest it goes up.

25 DAVIE: This is it. Now when ah pay him ah'm just clearing the interest. Ah'm no even touchin the original amount ah borrowed. Ah must have paid him back two or three times over, an ah still owe him the full whack.

BILLY: Bastard, eh? Sicken ye. And he's a pape.

(*DAVIE laughs*)

30 DAVIE: Still, aw ah need's a wee turn. Ah mean ma luck's got tae change sometime hasn't it? Law of averages.

BILLY: Whatever that is.

DAVIE: Thing's have got tae get better.

BILLY: It's a mug's game. The punter canny win.

DAVIE: Got tae keep trying.

35 BILLY: Flingin it away!

Look, don't get me wrong. Ah don't mind helping ye out, but I'm no exactly rollin in it maself.

DAVIE: Ye'll get yer money back.

BILLY: That's no what ah mean!

40 DAVIE: What am ah supposed tae dae? Get a job as a company director or something! Ah'll go doon tae the broo in the morning!

BILLY: There must be some way tae get this bookie aff yer back for a start.

DAVIE: Aye sure!

BILLY: Ah mean, you've paid him.

45 DAVIE: Ah knew his terms.

BILLY: It's no even legal.

DAVIE: Neither is getting his heavies tae kick folk's heids in.

BILLY: So maybe he's no the only wan that knows a few hard men.

DAVIE: (*Sighs*) Whit a carry on, eh?

MARKS

Questions

1. Referring to the whole extract, explain why Davie is having money problems. Make at least four key points.   **4**

2. What does the audience learn in lines 1-14 about the character of Billy?   **2**

3. Why does Davie laugh (line 28)?   **2**

4. Look closely at lines 29-49. Referring closely to the text, explain how this dialogue shows clearly the difference in outlook between Davie and Billy.   **4**

5. Money problems and ways to escape them are an important theme in *Sailmaker*. Referring briefly to the extract and in more detail to the rest of the play, explain how this theme is explored.   **8**

OR

SCOTTISH TEXT (PROSE)

Read the extract below and then attempt the following questions.

Question 2

The Cone-Gatherers **by Robin Jenkins**

This extract is from Chapter Five of the novel. Calum and Neil are high in a tree; they hear Duror starting to climb towards them.

They heard the scrapes and thumps of his nailed boots on the rungs and then on the branches. A branch cracked suddenly. He exclaimed as if in anger, and paused for a full minute. When he resumed he climbed even more slowly than before. Soon he stopped. He was still a long way below.

5 They waited, but he did not start to climb again. For three or four minutes they waited. Still he remained motionless and silent. One of the dogs barked unhappily.

They thought that he must have climbed as high as he wished and now was admiring the view of the loch. After all, the tree was not private just because they happened to be in it; the ladder, too, belonged to the estate. At the same time Neil felt curiously embarrassed
10 and could not think to start gathering cones again. Calum kept shivering.

They were far from guessing the truth, that Duror had ceased to climb because of fear; that weak and dizzy and full of shame, he was clinging with ignominious tightness; that the dread of the descent was making him sick; and that he had almost forgotten his purpose in ascending to them.

15 At last Neil had to end the suspense.

"Hello, Mr Duror," he called. "It's a grand day, isn't it?"

No reply came.

Neil tried again.

"Do you want to talk to us about something?" he shouted

20 This time, after another long delay, there was a reply. They were surprised by the mildness of his voice. It was so faint too they had to strain to hear it.

"I've got a message for you," he said.

"A message? Is it from Mr. Tulloch?"

There was a pause. "Aye, from him."

25 "Have we to go back home, to Ardmore?" cried Neil hopefully.

"You know these woods belong to Lady Runcie-Campbell?"

"We know that."

"She wants you as beaters in a deer drive this afternoon."

Neil was shocked.

30 "But we're here to gather cones," he yelled. "She can't order us about. She's not our mistress."

"She telephoned Tulloch. He said you've to work for her this afternoon."

"How could he? Didn't he tell us we'd to gather every cone we could? Didn't he ask us to work as much overtime as we liked? What's the good of all that if
35 we're to be taken away for deer drives." Neil's voice grew hoarse with indignation. "My brother's never asked to take part in deer hunts," he shouted. "Mr. Tulloch knows that. I don't believe he knows anything about this. It's just a trick to get us to work for the lady."

Duror was silent. His triumph was become a handful of withered leaves.
40 When he had seen the ladder, he had thought how gratifying it would be to deliver the deadly message to them in the eyrie where they fancied themselves safe. He had not anticipated this lightheadedness, this heaving of the stationary tree, this sickening of his very will to hate. He had never dreamed that he would not be able to do once only what the hunchback did
45 several times a day. It seemed to him that he must therefore be far more ill and decayed than he had thought. He was like a tree still straight, still showing green leaves; but underground death was creeping along the roots.

Questions

1. Summarise what happens in this extract from the novel. Make at least four key points.   **4**

2. How does the writer create a tense mood in lines 1–7?   **2**

3. Look carefully at what Neil says in lines 16–38. Referring closely to the text, show how his attitude to Duror goes through at least two changes.   **4**

4. Explain what the image in the final sentence tells you about Duror.   **2**

5. The deer drive, when it happens later, is a key turning point in the novel. Explain its importance to your understanding of a character or an important theme in the novel as a whole.   **8**

OR

SCOTTISH TEXT (PROSE)

Read the extract below and then attempt the following questions.

Question 3

Short stories by Anne Donovan

This extract is from the story "Away In A Manger".

They turned the corner and the cauld evaporated. The square shimmerin wi light, brightness sharp against the gloomy street. Trees frosted wi light. Lights shaped intae circles and flowers, like the plastic jewellery sets wee lassies love. Lights switchin on and off in a mad rhythm ae their ain, tryin tae look like bells ringin and snow fallin. Reindeer
5 and Santas, holly, ivy, robins, all bleezin wi light. Amy gazed at them, eyes shinin.

"Haud ma haund tae get across this road. There's lots of motors here." Sandra pulled Amy close tae her. "They're lovely aren't they?"

"Uh huh." Amy nodded. "Can we walk right round the square?"

A tape of Christmas carols was playin on the sound system, fillin the air like a cracklin
10 heavenly choir. Sandra and Amy joined the other faimlies wanderin round.

"Look at they reindeer, Mark!"

"There's a star, Daddy!"

"Check the size a that tree!"

Amy stopped in front of the big Christmas tree in the square.

15 "Can we sit doon tae look at it, Mammy?"

"Naw, just keep walkin', pet. It's too cauld."

Anyway, nearly every bench was occupied. Newspapers neatly smoothed oot like bedclothes. Some folk were huddled under auld coats, tryin tae sleep their way intae oblivion while others sat upright, hauf-empty cans in their haunds, starin at passers-by.
20 Sandra minded when she was wee and her mammy'd brought her tae see the lights. There were folk on benches then, down-and-outs, faces shrunk wi drink and neglect, an auld cap lyin hauf-heartedly by their sides. But now the people who slept in the square werenae just auld drunks and it was hard tae pick them oot fae everyone else. That couple ower there wi their bags roond them, were they just havin a rest fae their Christmas shoppin,
25 watchin the lights? But who in their right minds would be sittin on a bench in George Square on this freezing cauld night if they had a hame tae go tae?

Amy tugged at her airm. "Ah know that song."

"Whit song?"

"That one." Amy pointed upwards. "Silent Night, Holy Night."

MARKS

30   "Do you?"

"We learned it at school. Mrs Anderson was telling us aboot the baby Jesus and how there was nae room at the inn so he was born in a stable."

"Oh."

"It's no ma favourite, but."

35   "What's no your favourite?"

"Silent Night. Guess what ma favourite is?"

"Don't know."

"Guess, Mammy, you have tae guess."

Sandra couldnae be bothered guessin but she knew there'd be nae peace tae
40   she'd made some attempt and anyway, Amy'd get bored wi the "Guess what?" game quick enough.

"Little donkey?"

"Naw."

"O Little Town of Bethlehem?"

45   "Naw. Gie in?"

"OK."

"Away in a Manger. Ah've won!" Amy jumped up and doon. "Mammy, what's a manger?"

Questions

1. Show how the writer creates a mood of excitement in lines 1-10.   4

2. Why do you think lines 11-13 are included in the story at this point?   2

3. What difference does Sandra notice between the square now and what it was like when she went with her mother?   2

4. It what ways are lines 27-47 typical of an exchange between excited child and a parent?   4

5. Choose another story by Anne Donovan which focuses on a parent/child relationship and discuss its importance to that story.   8

OR

MARKS

SCOTTISH TEXT (POETRY)

Read the extract below and then attempt the following questions.

Question 4

Poems by Carol Ann Duffy

Anne Hathaway

Item: "I gyve unto my wife my second best bed ..."
(from Shakespeare's will)

The bed we loved in was a spinning world
of forests, castles, torchlight, clifftops, seas
where we would dive for pearls. My lover's words
were shooting stars which fell to earth as kisses
5 on these lips; my body now a softer rhyme
to his, now echo, assonance; his touch
a verb dancing in the centre of a noun.
Some nights, I dreamed he'd written me, the bed
a page beneath his writer's hands. Romance
10 and drama played by touch, by scent, by taste.
In the other bed, the best, our guests dozed on,
dribbling their prose. My living laughing love –
I hold him in the casket of my widow's head
as he held me upon that next best bed.

Questions

1. Referring to the section "The bed ..." to "... these lips" (lines 1-5), show how the poet conveys a sense of joy and happiness.   4

2. In lines 5-10, there are many references to writing poetry and plays.   Choose any two examples of this and explain in detail how each one adds to your understanding of the speaker's feelings.   4

3. Look closely at the last four lines (lines 11-14).

   (a) How does the poet makes clear how different the guests are from the speaker and her lover?   2

   (b) What feelings does the speaker show for her lover at the end of the poem?   2

4. Choose another poem by Carol Ann Duffy which explores the theme of love. Show how the poet explores the theme in your chosen poem.   8

[END OF PRACTICE QUESTION PAPER]

2013 Model Paper 2

N5

National
Qualifications
MODEL PAPER 2

English
Reading for Understanding, Analysis and Evaluation

Duration — 1 hour

Total marks — 30

When you are told to do so, open the booklet, read the passage and attempt all the questions, using your own words as far as possible.

The gr8 db8

Recently, a newspaper article headed "I h8 txt msgs: how texting is wrecking our language" argued that texters are "vandals who are doing to our language what Genghis Khan did to his neighbours 800 years ago. They are destroying it: pillaging our punctuation; savaging our sentences."

5   As a new variety of language, texting has been condemned as "textese", "slanguage", a "digital virus, "bleak, bald, sad shorthand", "drab shrinktalk which masks dyslexia, poor spelling and mental laziness".

Ever since the arrival of printing — thought to be the invention of the devil because it would put false opinions into people's minds — people have been arguing that new   technology   would   have disastrous consequences for language. Scares accompanied the introduction of the telegraph, the
10 telephone, and broadcasting. But has there ever been a linguistic phenomenon that has aroused such curiosity, suspicion, fear, confusion, antagonism, fascination, excitement and enthusiasm all at once as texting?

People think that the written language seen on mobile phone screens is new and alien, but all the popular beliefs about texting are wrong. Its distinctiveness is not a new phenomenon, nor is
15 its use restricted to the young. There is increasing evidence that it helps rather than hinders literacy. Texting has added a new dimension to language use, but its long-term impact is negligible.

Research has made it clear that the early media hysteria about the novelty (and thus the dangers) of text messaging was misplaced. People seem to have swallowed whole the stories
20 that youngsters use nothing but abbreviations when they text, such as the reports that a teenager had written an essay so full of textspeak that her teacher was unable to understand it. An extract was posted online, and quoted incessantly, but, as no one was ever able to track down the entire essay, it was probably a hoax.

There are several distinctive features of the way texts are written that combine to give the
25 impression of novelty, but people have been initialising common phrases for ages. IOU is known from 1618. There is no real difference between a modern kid's "lol" ("laughing out loud") and an earlier generation's "SWALK" ("sealed with a loving kiss").

English has had abbreviated words ever since it began to be written down. Words such as exam, vet, fridge and bus are so familiar that they have effectively become new words. When some of
30 these abbreviated forms first came into use, they also attracted criticism. In 1711, for example, Joseph Addison complained about the way words were being "miserably curtailed" — he mentioned pos (itive) and incog (nito).

Texters use deviant spellings — and they know they are deviant. But they are by no means the first to use such nonstandard forms as "cos" for "because" or "wot" for "what". Several of
35 these are so much part of English literary tradition that they have been given entries in the Oxford English Dictionary. "Cos" is there from 1828 and "wot" from 1829. Many can be found in the way dialect is written by such writers as Charles Dickens, Mark Twain, Walter Scott and D.H. Lawrence.

Sending a message on a mobile phone is not the most natural of ways to communicate. The
40 keypad isn't linguistically sensible. No one took letter-frequency considerations into account when designing it. For example, key 7 on my mobile contains four symbols, pqrs. It takes four key-presses to access the letter s, and yet s is one of the most frequently occurring letters in English. It is twice as easy to input q, which is one of the least frequently occurring letters. It should be the other way round. So any strategy that reduces the time and awkwardness of
45 inputting graphic symbols is bound to be attractive.

Abbreviations were used as a natural, intuitive response to a technological problem. And they appeared in next to no time. Texters simply transferred (and then embellished) what they had encountered in other settings. We have all left notes in which we have replaced "and" with "&", "three" with "3", and so on.

50 But the need to save time and energy is by no means the whole story of texting. When we look at some texts, they are linguistically quite complex. There are an extraordinary number of ways in which people play with language — creating riddles, solving crosswords, playing Scrabble, inventing new words. Professional writers do the same — providing catchy copy for advertising slogans, thinking up puns in newspaper headlines, and writing poems, novels and plays. Children
55 quickly learn that one of the most enjoyable things you can do with language is to play with its sounds, words, grammar — and spelling.

An extraordinary number of doom-laden prophecies have been made about the supposed linguistic evils unleashed by texting. Sadly, its creative potential has been virtually ignored. But children could not be good at texting if they had not already developed considerable literacy
60 awareness. Before you can write and play with abbreviated forms, you need to have a sense of how the sounds of your language relate to the letters. You need to know that there are such things as alternative spellings. If you are aware that your texting behaviour is different, you must have already realized that there is such a thing as a standard.

Some people dislike texting. Some are bemused by it. But it is merely the latest manifestation
65 of the human ability to be linguistically creative and to adapt language to suit the demands of diverse settings. There is no disaster pending. We will not see a new generation of adults growing up unable to write proper English. The language as a whole will not decline. In texting what we are seeing, in a small way, is language in evolution.

Adapted from an article by David Crystal in The Guardian.

MARKS

Questions

1. Choose any **two** examples of the language used to criticise texting in lines 1-6 and explain why each is effective in conveying disapproval.   **4**

2. Read lines 7-14.

   (a) What difference does the writer identify between the reaction to texting and the reaction to other new technologies?   **2**

   (b) Explain one way in which the writer's use of language in these lines conveys his surprise at the reaction to texting.   **2**

3. In lines 13–14 the writer says: "… all the popular beliefs about texting are wrong". **Explain in your own words** the evidence he provides for this in the rest of the paragraph.   **3**

4. Show how any **two** examples of the writer's word choice in lines 18-23 make clear his belief that the critics of texting are in the wrong.   **4**

5. Explain briefly how, in lines 24-38, the writer makes texting appear respectable.   **3**

6. Explain the function of each of the three dashes used in lines 50-56.   **3**

7. Show how any **two** examples of the writer's use of language in the last paragraph (lines 64-68) create a reassuring tone.   **4**

8. Referring to lines 24-63, summarise **in your own words** the key reasons not to worry about texting.   **5**

[END OF PRACTICE QUESTION PAPER]

N5

National
Qualifications
MODEL PAPER 2

English
Critical Reading

Duration — 1 hour and 30 minutes

Total marks — 40

SECTION 1 — 20 marks

Write ONE critical essay on a previously studied text from Drama, Prose, Poetry, Film and TV Drama or Language Study.

SECTION 2 — 20 marks

Read an extract from a Scottish text you have previously studied and attempt the questions.

You should spend approximately 45 minutes on each section.

SECTION 1 — CRITICAL ESSAY — 30 marks

Attempt ONE question from this section of the paper from ONE of the Parts A–E.

You may use a Scottish text but <u>not</u> the one used in Section 2.

Your essay should be on a different <u>genre</u> to the one used in Section 2.

Write the number of your chosen question in the margin of your answer.

You should spend about 45 minutes on the essay.

PART A — DRAMA

Answers to questions in this part should refer to the text and to such relevant features as characterisation, key scene(s), structure, climax, theme, plot, conflict, setting . . .

1. Choose a play in which there is a character who suffers from a human weakness such as ambition, selfishness, lack of self-knowledge, jealousy, pride, lust . . .

   By referring to appropriate techniques, show how the weakness is revealed, and then explain how this weakness affects both the characters and the events of the play.

2. Choose a play which you feel has a dramatic final scene.

   Describe briefly what happens in the final scene and then, by referring to appropriate techniques, explain how effective the ending is in bringing to a conclusion the central concerns of the text.

PART B — PROSE

Answers to questions in this part should refer to the text and to such relevant features as characterisation, setting, language, key incident(s), climax, turning point, plot, structure, narrative technique, theme, ideas, description . . .

3. Choose a novel **or** short story with an ending which you find satisfactory.

   By referring to appropriate techniques, explain why you find the ending satisfactory in bringing to a conclusion the main concerns of the text as a whole.

4. Choose a novel **or** a short story **or** a work of non-fiction which deals with an important human issue (such as the abuse of power, conflict between good and evil, loss of freedom or hatred between individuals or groups).

   By referring to appropriate techniques, show how the author reveals the issue through the portrayal of people and events throughout the text, and show how your understanding of the issue has deepened.

PART C — POETRY

> *Answers to questions in this part should refer to the text and to such relevant features as word choice, tone, imagery, structure, content, rhythm, rhyme, theme, sound, ideas . . .*

5. Choose a poem in which the poet creates a particular mood or atmosphere.

   By referring to appropriate techniques, show how the poet creates this mood **or** atmosphere.

6. Choose a poem which could be considered as having a powerful message.

   By referring to appropriate techniques, show how the poet effectively conveys this message.

PART D — FILM AND TV DRAMA

> *Answers to questions in this part should refer to the text and to such relevant features as use of camera, key sequence, characterisation, mise-en-scène, editing, setting, music/ sound, special effects, plot, dialogue . . .*

7. Choose a film **or** TV drama* which creates suspense or tension either in a particular scene **or** throughout the whole film or TV drama.

   By referring to appropriate techniques, show how the suspense or tension is created and how it affects your enjoyment of the film or TV drama as a whole.

8. Choose a film **or** TV drama* which both entertains and helps to raise awareness of social issues.

   By referring to appropriate techniques, show how the film or TV drama you have chosen succeeds in both these aspects.

* "TV drama" includes a single play, a series or a serial.

PART E — LANGUAGE STUDY

> *Answers to questions in this part should refer to the text and to such relevant features as register, accent, dialect, slang, jargon, vocabulary, tone, abbreviation . . .*

9. Consider the specialist language used by any group of people to talk about a particular interest, for example, a sport, a job, a hobby . . .

   By referring to specific examples and to appropriate features of language, show how the specialist language used by the group is effective in communicating ideas clearly.

10. Consider how TV programmes aimed at young audiences have an effect on the language young people use.

    Identify any recent changes in vocabulary or accent that you are aware of and, by referring to specific examples and to appropriate features of language, explain whether you feel the new words/accents are more effective in communicating than those which they have replaced.

SECTION 2 – SCOTTISH TEXT – 20 marks

Attempt only ONE question from ONE of the three parts (Drama, Prose or Poetry).

You must choose a different genre to the text you used in Section 1.

You should spend about 45 minutes on this question.

Read the extract carefully and then attempt ALL the questions below the extract, using your own words as far as possible.

SCOTTISH TEXT (DRAMA)

Read the extract below and then attempt the following questions.

Question 1

Tally's Blood by Ann Marie di Mambro

This extract is from Act Two, Scene Two, in the back shop.

	ROSINELLA:	You like Silvio Palombo, don't you?
	LUCIA:	He's okay.
	ROSINELLA:	Nice looking boy too.
	LUCIA:	He's okay.
5	ROSINELLA:	Oh, come on, Lucia, you can't kid me on. I know you're daft for him. But I like the way you kind of stand back a bit – don't let him see you're too keen. Italian boys like that. Don't want him to get fed up waiting.
	LUCIA:	Auntie Rosinella…?
10	ROSINELLA:	He cannae keep his eyes off you. And if he's who you want, then it's not for me to stand in your way. But I told his mother. I made sure I told her. 'Mrs Palombo', I said, 'our Lucia's a lady. She's not been brought up to work in a shop, running after some man'. I tell you, Lucia, she liked me for that. They've got class that family.
	LUCIA:	Auntie Rosinella…?
15	ROSINELLA:	I hear them all the time. 'Ma lassie's an awfy good worker' – 'Ma lassie cleaned four chickens' – I promised myself – my Lucia's to marry a man that really loves HER – no to put her in a shop and make her work. How much you got there?
	LUCIA:	Three pounds, seven and tenpence ha'penny.
20	ROSINELLA:	That's what I want for you – a good life – with a good Italian man – here.
	LUCIA:	Auntie Rosinella…?

ROSINELLA: You see the way the Italians are getting on now, eh? Beginning to make a wee bit money? Because they're prepared to WORK that's why. I don't know anybody works so hard as the Italian men.

25   *Hughie in with pail and mop.*

HUGHIE: That's the tables cleared and the front shop mopped, Mrs Pedreschi, and the chip pan cleaned out. Is the milk boiled?

ROSINELLA: Should be.

30   *She turns attention back to Lucia, Hughie lifts pot from stove and pours contents into two pails; he covers them and sets them aside, working like a Trojan.*

ROSINELLA: And the way they love their families. Nobody loves their families like the Italians! You want to stay for a wee bit pasta, Hughie? It's your favourite – Rigatoni.

35   HUGHIE: No thanks, Mrs Pedreschi. I better get up the road. Bridget's going out and I don't like my mammy left on her own.

ROSINELLA: Bridget's going out is she? Don't tell me she's winching?

HUGHIE: No. Her and Davie are going up to Charmaine's the night – to go over all the arrangements. My mammy's no up to it.

40   ROSINELLA: That's right. When's the wedding now?

HUGHIE: Saturday.

ROSINELLA: Is he no getting married a wee bit quick, your brother?

             Hughie shrugs, a bit embarrassed: Lucia mortified at Rosinella.

ROSINELLA: And where are they going to stay?

45   HUGHIE: At Charmaine's.

ROSINELLA: It's funny that, isn't it? But that's the way they do it here. In Italy, the girl must go to her husband's house. That's why you must have land if you've got sons.

             Massimo in.

50   So that'll be your mammy left with her eldest and her youngest, eh? I don't see your Bridget ever marrying, do you? You see, Lucia, there's a lot of women Bridget's age no' married. The war killed that many young men. I'm right there, aren't I, Massimo?

MASSIMO: You got those pails ready, son?

55   HUGHIE: I'll bring them through.

      MASSIMO: And give's a hand to put these shutters up before you go.

      Hughie and Massimo out: Rosinella watches him go.

      ROSINELLA: I'm right about that Davie, amn't I, Lucia? Give it five or six
60   months, Hughie'll be telling us he's an uncle again. Mind
                   you, I suppose his mother must feel it, right enough. Can
                   you find me a wee envelope hen, a wee poke or something?
                   What was I saying… ah, yes… See what I mean about Italian
                   men? Just take that brother of Hughie's. Getting married on
                   a Saturday. Give him two or three days and he'll be out
65   DRINKING with his pals.

                   *Rosinella shushes up when Hughie comes in, followed by
                   Massimo: all locked up. Massimo takes off his apron, reaches for a
                   bottle of wine.*

      MASSIMO: Thanks, Hughie, son. You want a wee glass of wine?

70   HUGHIE: I better not, Mr Pedreschi. I better get up the road.

Questions

1. Read lines 1-19.

   (a) Show how the playwright makes the audience aware of **two** aspects of
       Rosinella's character.   4

   (b) How is the audience made aware of Lucia's lack of interest in what her
       aunt is saying?   2

2. In lines 20-70 Rosinella displays a number of prejudices. Explain how the
   playwright makes the audience aware of how silly her prejudices are. Refer to
   at least three different prejudices.   6

3. Explain how Rosinella overcomes her prejudices in the course of the play as a
   whole.   8

OR

SCOTTISH TEXT (PROSE)

Read the extract below and then attempt the following questions.

Question 2

Kidnapped **by Robert Louis Stevenson**

This extract is from Chapter 10 - "The Siege of the Roundhouse".

The sea had gone down, and the wind was steady and kept the sails quiet; so that there was a great stillness in the ship, in which I made sure I heard the sound of muttering voices. A little after, and there came a clash of steel upon the deck, by which I knew they were dealing out the cutlasses and one had been let fall; and after that, silence again.

5   I do not know if I was what you call afraid; but my heart beat like a bird's, both quick and little; and there was a dimness came before my eyes which I continually rubbed away, and which continually returned. As for hope, I had none; but only a darkness of despair and a sort of anger against all the world that made me long to sell my life as dear as I was able. I tried to pray, I remember, but that same hurry of my mind, like a man running, would not
10 suffer me to think upon the words; and my chief wish was to have the thing begin and be done with it.

It came all of a sudden when it did, with a rush of feet and a roar, and then a shout from Alan, and a sound of blows and some one crying out as if hurt. I looked back over my shoulder, and saw Mr. Shuan in the doorway, crossing blades with Alan.

15 "That's him that killed the boy!" I cried.

"Look to your window!" said Alan; and as I turned back to my place, I saw him pass his sword through the mate's body.

It was none too soon for me to look to my own part; for my head was scarce back at the window, before five men, carrying a spare yard for a battering-ram, ran past me and took
20 post to drive the door in. I had never fired with a pistol in my life, and not often with a gun; far less against a fellow-creature. But it was now or never; and just as they swang the yard, I cried out: "Take that!" and shot into their midst.

I must have hit one of them, for he sang out and gave back a step, and the rest stopped as if a little disconcerted. Before they had time to recover, I sent another ball over their heads;
25 and at my third shot (which went as wide as the second) the whole party threw down the yard and ran for it.

Then I looked round again into the deck-house. The whole place was full of the smoke of my own firing, just as my ears seemed to be burst with the noise of the shots. But there was Alan, standing as before; only now his sword was running blood to the hilt, and
30 himself so swelled with triumph and fallen into so fine an attitude, that he looked to be invincible. Right before him on the floor was Mr. Shuan, on his hands and knees; the blood was pouring from his mouth, and he was sinking slowly lower, with a terrible, white face; and just as I looked, some of those from behind caught hold of him by the heels and dragged him bodily out of the round-house. I believe he died as they were doing it.

MARKS

35   "There's one of your Whigs for ye!" cried Alan; and then turning to me, he asked if I had done much execution.

I told him I had winged one, and thought it was the captain.

"And I've settled two," says he. "No, there's not enough blood let; they'll be back again. To your watch, David. This was but a dram before meat."

Questions

1. Show how Stevenson creates a tense atmosphere in lines 1-4.   3

2. What mixed emotions does David feel in lines 5-11?   2

3. Explain briefly **three** ways by which Stevenson makes the events in lines 12-26 dramatic and exciting.   3

4. What impressions is the reader given of Alan Breck in lines 27-39?   2

5. "This was but a dram before meat" (line 39). Explain in your own words what Alan means by this.   2

6. David's relationship with Alan Breck is a very important aspect of *Kidnapped*. Referring to other parts of the novel, describe how the relationship changes in the course of story.   8

OR

SCOTTISH TEXT (PROSE)

Read the extract below and then attempt the following questions.

Question 3

Short stories by Iain Crichton Smith

This extract is from the story "In Church".

"At the age of eighteen I was forced into the army to fight for what they call one's country. I did not know what this was since my gaze was always directed inward and not outward. I was put among men whom I despised and feared – they fornicated and drank and spat and lived filthily. Yet they were my comrades in arms.

5 "I was being shot at by strangers. I was up to my knees in green slime. I was harassed by rats. I entered trenches to find the dead buried in the walls. Once, however, on a clear starry night at Christmas time we had a truce. This lasted into the following day. We – Germans and English – showed each other our photographs, though I had none. We, that is, the others, played football. At the end of it a German officer came up to us and said:
10 "You had better get back to your dugouts: we are starting a barrage at 13.00 hours." He consulted his watch and we went back to our trenches after he had shaken hands with each other.

"One day I could bear no more of the killing and I ran away. And I came here, Lord. And now I should like to say something to you, Lord. I was never foolish enough to think that
15 I understood your ways. Nevertheless I thought you were on the side of the good and the innocent. Now I no longer believe so. You may strike me dead with your lightning – I invite you to do so – but I think that will not happen. All these years, Lord, you have cheated me. You in your immense absence." He paused a moment as if savouring the phrase. "Your immense absence. As for me, I have been silent for a year without love,
20 without hope. I have lived like an animal, I who was willing to give my all to you. Lord, do you know what it is to be alone? For in order to live we need language and human beings.

"I think, Lord, that I hate you. I hate you for inventing the world and then abandoning it. I hate you because you have not intervened to save the world.

25 "I hate you because you are as indifferent as the generals. I hate you because of my weakness.

"I hate you, God, because of what you have done to mankind."

He stopped and looked at Colin as if he were asking him, Am I a good preacher or not?

"You have said," said Colin after a long time, "exactly what I would have said. "I have no
30 wish to …"

"Betray me? But you are an officer. It is your duty. What else can you do?"

MARKS

Questions

1. Explain briefly what has led up to this moment in the story, and say what happens immediately after it.   **4**

2. How do any **two** examples of the writer's use of language in lines 1-4 make clear the speaker's dislike for the army?   **2**

3. Explain one way in which the writer uses contrast in lines 5-12 to emphasise the strangeness of the Christmas truce.   **2**

4. Explain your own words why the speaker is angry at God.   **4**

5. Many of Crichton Smith's short stories have unexpected endings. Choose another of his stories which has this type of ending, and discuss whether or not you find the ending satisfactory.   **8**

OR

SCOTTISH TEXT (POETRY)

Read the extract below and then attempt the following questions.

Question 4

Poems by Norman MacCaig

Visiting Hour

The hospital smell
combs my nostrils
as they go bobbing along
green and yellow corridors.

5 What seems a corpse
is trundled into a lift and vanishes
heavenward.

I will not feel, I will not
feel, until
10 I have to.

Nurses walk lightly, swiftly,
here and up and down and there,
their slender waists miraculously
carrying their burden
15 of so much pain, so
many deaths, their eyes
still clear after
so many farewells.

Ward 7.
20 She lies
in a white cave of forgetfulness.
A withered hand
trembles on its stalk. Eyes move
behind eyelids too heavy
25 to raise. Into an arm wasted
of colour a glass fang is fixed,
not guzzling but giving.
And between her and me
distance shrinks till there is none left
30 but the distance of pain that neither she nor I
can cross.

(continued overleaf)

She smiles a little at this
black figure in her white cave
who clumsily rises
35 in the round swimming waves of a bell
and dizzily goes off, growing fainter,
not smaller, leaving behind only
books that will not be read
and fruitless fruits.

Questions

1. Explain how the speaker's sense of discomfort is conveyed in lines 1-10.   **4**

2. What is the speaker's attitude to the nurses (lines 11-18)? Refer to the text to support your answer.   **2**

3. Choose **two** examples of imagery from lines 19-31 and explain in detail how each one adds to your understanding of the poem.   **4**

4. "...leaving behind only
   books that will not be read
   and fruitless fruits."

   Do you think this is a good way to end the poem? Justify your answer.   **2**

5. "Visiting Hour" is a deeply personal and emotional poem. Choose a similar poem by MacCaig and explain how he conveys strong emotions in that poem.   **8**

[END OF PRACTICE QUESTION PAPER]

National
Qualifications
MODEL PAPER 3

English
Reading for Understanding, Analysis and Evaluation

Duration — 1 hour

Total marks — 30

When you are told to do so, open the booklet, read the passage and attempt all the questions, using your own words as far as possible.

HODDER
GIBSON
LEARN MORE

Why Dickens was the hero of Soweto

In this passage, the writer informs us about the effect that books by Charles Dickens, a 19th-century English writer, had on black South African children during the time of racial segregation ("apartheid") in South Africa. "Afrikaans" is the language which was spoken in South Africa by the white rulers before the arrival of democracy in that country.

Hector Pieterson was 12 when he died. Today a museum bearing his name commemorates his death — and hundreds of others — which occurred some 30 years ago at a place whose name has come to symbolise uprising against oppression: Soweto.

5   Hector was one of thousands of black children who took to the streets on June 16, 1976, in protest about schooling under the apartheid regime in South Africa. When police opened fire on the march it brought the word Soweto to the attention of the world. But less well known is the role that Charles Dickens played in events.

The march was in protest at a government edict making Afrikaans compulsory in schools. From January 1976, half of all subjects were to be taught in it, including ones in which difficulties of 10   translation were often an issue.

To pupils accustomed to being educated in English, the Afrikaans policy was the last of a line insults delivered in the name of "Bantu" or "negative education". They thought being taught in Afrikaans, the language of a regime that had tried to "unpeople" them, would cost them their last remaining freedom — that of thinking for themselves, using their minds.

15   That is where Dickens came in. Many books were banned under apartheid but not the classics of English literature. Pupils arriving hungry at school every day were captivated by the story of a frail but courageous boy named Oliver Twist.

The book was a revelation. Systemised oppression of children happened in England too! They were not alone. Slave labour, thin rations and cruel taunts were part of a child's life in the 20   world outside as well.

One former pupil, now in his forties, says of Dickens: "Four or five of us would be together and discuss the stories. And to think he wasn't banned! The authorities didn't know what was in these books, how they helped us to be strong, to think that we were not forgotten."

Not being forgotten was particularly crucial. The apartheid regime had tried to "vanish" black 25   people. Feeling abandoned and isolated, people turned to Dickens as someone who understood their plight.

But there were not enough books to go round. Few of the crateloads of Shakespeare, Hardy and Dickens shipped from Britain reached the townships. Instead, they came to Soweto in parcels from charities. They were read by candlelight, often out loud, shared in a circle, or passed from 30   hand to hand.

At Morrris Isaacson School, one of the moving forces behind the Soweto protest, which produced two of its leaders, Murphy Morobe, "Shakespeare's best friend in Africa", and Tsietsi Mashinini, there were 1,500 pupils and three copies of *Oliver Twist* in 1976. The former pupils recall waiting months for their turn, with a similar wait for *Nicholas Nickleby*.

35   But it was Oliver that they took to heart: students at one of the country's leading black colleges, Lovedale, formed a committee to ask for more.

Calling it the Board, after Dicken's Board of Guardians, they asked for more lessons, more food — and more and better books. Their reward was to be charged with public violence. All 152 "board" members were expelled from the college and some were jailed.

They felt that Dickens was obviously on their side. Descriptions of Gamfield's "ugly leer" and
40 Bumble's "repulsive countenance" and Oliver being beaten by Mrs Sowerberry and shoved "but nothing daunted" into the dust-cellar were evidence that this English author understood the plight of black South Africans.

Dickens's compassion for the poor linked the people of Soweto to a worldwide literature of tremendous importance.

45 The veteran South African trumpeter Hugh Masekela later chose *Nicholas Nickleby* as his favourite book on a popular radio programme, *Desert Island Discs*, telling the presenter what its author did for people in the townships: "He taught us suffering is the same everywhere."

The love of books that enabled an author dead for more than 100 years to inspire thousands of schoolchildren came mainly from grandmothers who had educated their families orally, then
50 urged them to read widely and learn all that they could.

It also came from people such as the activist Steve Biko, whose own mentor, the Brazilian educator Paulo Freire, spent a lifetime working with forest people who had no formal education, teaching them to "name the world their own way".

That is what the youth of Soweto wanted — a future in their own words. And they got it. By the
55 following year, Afrikaans had been withdrawn from classrooms as unworkable. And so, thanks to the influence of a long-dead British author, the sacrifices of Hector Pieterson and many other Africans have proved to be not entirely in vain — which Dickens himself would surely applaud.

Adapted from an article by Carol Lee in The Times.

MARKS

Questions

1. Explain fully any **two** ways in which the writer makes the opening paragraph dramatic.   4

2. Referring to lines 1-14, explain **in your own words** why Sowetans were protesting.   3

3. Why, according to the writer in lines 15-26, was the story of Oliver Twist so popular among young Sowetans?   4

4. Show how any **two** examples of the writer's word choice in lines 15-20 create sympathy for the character Oliver Twist.   4

5. Explain the function of the colon in line 35.   2

6. Referring to lines 27-47, summarise **in your own words** the key evidence the writer uses to show Dickens' popularity among black South Africans.   4

7. What does the paragraph in lines 37-39 suggest about the Government in South Africa at the time?   2

8. Read lines 48-57.

   (a) Explain briefly how each paragraph shows the importance various groups of people attach to education.   3

   (b) Show how any **two** examples of the writers' use of language in these lines create a very positive and inspiring conclusion to the passage.   4

[END OF PRACTICE QUESTION PAPER]

National
Qualifications
MODEL PAPER 3

English
Critical Reading

Duration — 1 hour and 30 minutes

Total marks — 40

SECTION 1 — 20 marks

Write ONE critical essay on a previously studied text from Drama, Prose, Poetry, Film and TV Drama or Language Study.

SECTION 2 — 20 marks

Read an extract from a Scottish text you have previously studied and attempt the questions.

You should spend approximately 45 minutes on each section.

HODDER
GIBSON
LEARN MORE

SECTION 1 — CRITICAL ESSAY — 30 marks

Attempt ONE question from this section of the paper from ONE of the Parts A-E.

You may use a Scottish text but <u>not</u> the one used in Section 2.

Your essay should be on a different <u>genre</u> to the one used in Section 2.

Write the number of your chosen question in the margin of your answer.

You should spend about 45 minutes on the essay.

PART A — DRAMA

> *Answers to questions in this part should refer to the text and to such relevant features as characterisation, key scene(s), structure, climax, theme, plot, conflict, setting . . .*

1. Choose a play in which one of the main concerns is love **or** jealousy **or** betrayal **or** reconciliation.

   Explain what the concern is, and by referring to appropriate techniques show how it is explored throughout the play.

2. Choose a scene from a play in which suspense or tension is built up.

   By referring to appropriate techniques, show how this suspense or tension is built up and what effect this scene has on the play as a whole.

PART B — PROSE

> *Answers to questions in this part should refer to the text and to such relevant features as characterisation, setting, language, key incident(s), climax, turning point, plot, structure, narrative technique, theme, ideas, description . . .*

3. Choose a novel **or** a short story in which a character is in conflict with his or her friends or relatives or society.

   By referring to appropriate techniques, show how the conflict arises and what effect it has on the character's fate in the novel or short story as a whole.

4. Choose a novel **or** a short story **or** a work of non-fiction in which setting is an important feature.

   By referring to appropriate techniques, explain how the writer creates the setting, and then go on to show how this feature contributes to your understanding of the text as a whole.

PART C — POETRY

> *Answers to questions in this part should refer to the text and to such relevant features as word choice, tone, imagery, structure, content, rhythm, rhyme, theme, sound, ideas . . .*

5. Choose a poem which reflects on an aspect of human behaviour in such a way as to deepen your understanding of human nature.

   Describe the aspect of human behaviour which you have identified and, by referring to appropriate techniques, show how the poem brought you to a deeper understanding of human nature.

6. Choose a poem which portrays an interesting character.

   By referring to appropriate techniques, show how the poet makes the character interesting.

PART D — FILM AND TV DRAMA

> *Answers to questions in this part should refer to the text and to such relevant features as use of camera, key sequence, characterisation, mise-en-scène, editing, setting, music/sound, special effects, plot, dialogue . . .*

7. Choose a film **or** TV drama* in which the main character is an individual for whom we feel sympathy.

   By referring to appropriate techniques, show how the character is portrayed in such a way that we feel sympathy.

8. Choose an opening sequence from a film which effectively holds your interest and makes you want to watch the rest of the film.

   By referring to appropriate techniques, show what elements of the opening sequence have this effect, and how they relate to the film as a whole.

* "TV drama" includes a single play, a series or a serial.

PART E — LANGUAGE STUDY

> *Answers to questions in this part should refer to the text and to such relevant features as register, accent, dialect, slang, jargon, vocabulary, tone, abbreviation . . .*

9. Consider the ways that young people use the internet to communicate and socialise, for example: social networking sites, instant messaging, chat rooms, blogs . . .

   By referring to specific examples and to appropriate features of language, explain how such communication differs from formal English, and what its attractions are for young people.

10. Consider a text which you find to be persuasive, for example: an advertisement, a speech, a newspaper article . . .

    By referring to specific examples and to appropriate features of language, show how persuasive techniques have been used to convince you.

SECTION 2 — SCOTTISH TEXT — 20 marks

Attempt only ONE question from ONE of the three parts (Drama, Prose or Poetry).

You must choose a different genre to the text you used in Section 1.

You should spend about 45 minutes on this question.

Read the extract carefully and then attempt ALL the questions below the extract, using your own words as far as possible.

SCOTTISH TEXT (DRAMA)

Read the extract below and then attempt the following questions.

Question 1

Bold Girls by Rona Munro

This extract is from Scene 2 in the Club. Cassie is dancing alone, and Nora persuades Marie to join her.

        Marie crosses over and joins Cassie, who beams, applauding her. Marie starts shuffling cautiously from foot to foot.

CASSIE: I'm telling you this is a great diet Marie, you really feel the benefit of the gin.

MARIE: Well maybe you should go easy now Cassie.

5   CASSIE: Oh I'm a long way from being lockjawed

        Nora is beckoning at them frantically.

MARIE: Your mummy's asking us to come and sit down.

CASSIE: The song's just started.

        Marie glances round nervously.

10   What? Are they all watching us?

MARIE: They are.

CASSIE: Let them.

MARIE: (*with a shaky laugh*): Feel a bit like the last meat pie in the shop out here, Cassie.

CASSIE: Well let them stay hungry. They can just look and think what they like.

15   MARIE: Cassie, what's wrong?

CASSIE: Oh, I'm just bad, Marie, didn't you know?

	MARIE:	No. I never knew that.
	CASSIE:	You remember that wee girl in Turf Lodge, the one Martin couldn't get enough of? She was a decent wee girl. She's bad now. Ask my mummy.
20	MARIE:	Have you had words?
	CASSIE:	He's out in less than a year, Marie.
	MARIE:	*Martin!?*
	CASSIE:	Joe.
	MARIE:	I know. It'll be all right Cassie.
25		*They stop dancing, they look at each other.*
	MARIE:	It'll be all right, Cassie.
	CASSIE:	I tell you Marie I can't stand the *smell* of him. The greasy, grinning, beer bellied smell of him. And he's winking away about all he's been dreaming of, wriggling his fat fingers over me like I'm a poke of chips – I don't want
30		him in the house in my *bed*, Marie.
	MARIE:	You'll cope.
	CASSIE:	Oh I'm just bad. I am.
	MARIE:	Don't. Don't say that about yourself.
	CASSIE:	I'll go crazy.
35	MARIE:	I won't let you. You won't get a chance Cassie, I'll just be across the road, I won't let you go crazy. You just see what you'll get if you try it.

Slowly Cassie smiles at her.

(*Putting a hand on Cassie's arm*) Now will you come and sit down?

MARKS

Questions

1. Show how the playwright contrasts the characters of Marie and Cassie through their language and their actions in lines 1-14.   4

2. Explain how the dialogue in lines 15-38 reveals aspects of the relationship between Marie and Cassie.   4

3. Referring closely to the language of lines 27-30 show how Cassie reveals her attitude to Joe.   4

4. The relationship between Marie and Cassie is central to Bold Girls. Referring briefly to the extract and in more detail to the rest of the play, explain how this relationship develops.   8

OR

SCOTTISH TEXT (PROSE)

Read the extract below and then attempt the following questions.

Question 2

The Testament of Gideon Mack by James Robertson
This extract is from Chapter 7 of the novel.

Another few minutes must have gone by. I forgot where I was and what day it was. The sound was louder than I'd intended. I was only a foot away from the screen, finger hovering near the off switch, and maybe that was why I failed to hear my father's footsteps in the hall. By the time the door opened and his voice filled the room – "Agnes?
5 I thought I heard somebody …" – there was no point in even bothering to switch the television off. I did, though, and jumped to my feet in a flush of shame and fury.

He closed the door behind him. I stood between him and the television set as if to protect it, as if to say it was not to blame. I could see the wee flames in his cheeks. I bowed my head, fixing my eye on a crack in the skirting board. I heard him say, "Put it back on."

10 "No, no, it doesn't matter, I'm sorry," I mumbled. Entirely the wrong thing. He cut me off, his voice shaking.

"It doesn't *matter*?" he said "Do you dare to disobey me? Put it back on."

I turned and reached for the switch. The television, being warm, came on at once. If my father understood that, he made no allowance for it.

15 "I see you have become very skilled at operating that thing," he said quietly, almost admiringly. "How often have you done this?"

"Never," I said. It was true that I'd not touched the set before on a Sunday. "I promise this is the first time."

"It will be the last," he said. "Come here."

20 He pointed beside him and I went and stood there. His huge right hand descended on my neck and the thumb and fingers gripped it so that I cried out. He increased the pressure. I thought my head would snap off. His breathing was like that of some monstrous creature in its den. The blood in his fingers pulsed furiously against my neck.

Thus we stood in front of the television together, father and son, for the remaining ten
25 minutes of the programme. It felt like an hour. If I squirmed to try and ease the pain, his grip tightened. I hated him then, hated what he was doing to me and hated my own helplessness. *ZAP! BLAM! POW!* I hated the screen with its cartoon punches and I hated the way the parlour echoed with screeching tyres and wisecracks delivered in American accents. I saw it as if through his eyes – cheap, tawdry, meaningless rubbish – and I
30 longed for it to end.

He pushed me from him as the credits rolled and the inane theme music played. "Turn it off," he said. I did as I was told, rubbing my neck and wiping away the tears that he had squeezed out of me.

"What ... is ... that?" he said, dropping the words methodically into the silence.

35 "*Batman*," I said.

"Bat ... man," he said.

"Yes," I said. And then again, "I'm sorry." But I don't think he heard that.

"It is not bat ... man," he said, and I could not stop myself, I was trying to explain, I said, "It *is*."

40 "Do not interrupt me," he said. His voice grew louder and louder. "Do not contradict me. It is not bat ... man, whatever that means. I'll tell you what it is. It is drivel. It is the most unutterable garbage I have ever witnessed. Garbage from the land of garbage."

Questions

1. Summarise what happens in this extract. Make **three** key points.   **3**

2. How is the reader made aware, in lines 1-11, of Gideon's nervousness after he hears his father's voice?   **2**

3. Explain how the writer conveys the aggressiveness of Gideon's father in lines 12-33.   **4**

4. How is the father's contempt for American culture conveyed in lines 34-44?   **3**

5. This incident is an important one in the development of Gideon's character. Choose another important incident from the novel, explain briefly what happens in it and go on to show why it is important in the development of Gideon's character.   **8**

OR

SCOTTISH TEXT (POETRY)

Read the extract below and then attempt the following questions.

Question 3

Poems by Jackie Kay

Lucozade

My mum is on a high bed next to sad chrysanthemums.
'Don't bring flowers, they only wilt and die.'
I am scared my mum is going to die
on the bed next to the sad chrysanthemums.

5   She nods off and her eyes go back in her head.
Next to her bed is a bottle of Lucozade.
'Orange nostalgia, that's what that is,' she says.
'Don't bring Lucozade either,' then fades.

'The whole day was a blur, a swarm of eyes.
10 Those doctors with their white lies.
Did you think you could cheer me up with a *Woman's Own*?
Don't bring magazines, too much about size.'

My mum wakes up, groggy and low.
'What I want to know,' she says, 'is this:
15 where's the big brandy, the generous gin, the Bloody Mary,
the biscuit tin, the chocolate gingers, the dirty big meringue?'

I am sixteen; I've never tasted a Bloody Mary.
'Tell your father to bring a luxury,' says she.
'Grapes have no imagination, they're just green.
20 Tell him: stop the neighbours coming.'

I clear her cupboard in Ward 10B, Stobhill Hospital.
I leave, bags full, Lucozade, grapes, oranges,
sad chrysanthemums under my arms,
weighted down. I turn round, wave with her flowers.

25 My mother, on her high hospital bed, waves back.
Her face is light and radiant, dandelion hours.
Her sheets billow and whirl. She is beautiful.
Next to her the empty table is divine.

I carry the orange nostalgia home singing an old song.

MARKS

Questions

1. The poet twice refers to Lucozade as "orange nostalgia". What does she mean by this?   **2**

2. Briefly describe the mother's mood in lines 1-12.   **2**

3. Explain fully how the poet contrasts "grapes" with the "luxury" the mother asks for.   **4**

4. Describe the speaker's mood in lines 21-29 and explain in detail how it is conveyed.   **4**

5. Relationships between generations is a common theme in Jackie Kay's poetry. Choose another poem by her which explores this theme and explain how she does so.   **8**

OR

SCOTTISH TEXT (POETRY)

Read the extract below and then attempt the following questions.

Question 4

Poems by Edwin Morgan

Trio

Coming up Buchanan Street, quickly, on a sharp winter evening
a young man and two girls, under the Christmas lights –
The young man carries a new guitar in his arms,
the girl on the inside carries a very young baby,
5 and the girl on the outside carries a chihuahua.
And the three of them are laughing, their breath rises
in a cloud of happiness, and as they pass
the boy says, "Wait till he sees this but!"
The chihuahua has a tiny Royal Stewart tartan coat like a teapot-
10   holder,
the baby in its white shawl is all bright eyes and mouth like favours
        in a fresh sweet cake,
the guitar swells out under its milky plastic cover, tied at the neck
        with silver tinsel tape and a brisk sprig of mistletoe.
15 Orphean sprig! Melting baby! Warm chihuahua!
The vale of tears is powerless before you.
Whether Christ is born, or is not born, you
put paid to fate, it abdicates
                under the Christmas lights.
20 Monsters of the year
go blank, are scattered back,
can't bear this march of three.

– And the three have passed, vanished in the crowd
(yet not vanished, for in their arms they wind
25 the life of men and beasts, and music,
laughter ringing them round like a guard)
at the end of this winter's day.

MARKS

Questions

1. Explain briefly how the poet establishes a happy mood in lines 1-8.   **2**

2. Look at the descriptions in lines 9-14 of the chihuahua, the baby, and the guitar. Choose any **two** of these and explain in detail how the poet's use of language creates an effective description.   **4**

3. In lines 15-22 the poet gives his thoughts about what he has just seen. In your own words, explain what he says.   **4**

4. Describe the poet's mood in the final stanza (lines 23-27).   **2**

5. In this poem, Morgan takes an everyday, ordinary situation and transforms it into something special and thought-provoking. Choose another poem by him in which he does the same thing and explain how he adds significance to an ordinary event.   **8**

[END OF PRACTICE QUESTION PAPER]

NATIONAL 5 | ANSWER SECTION

SQA AND HODDER GIBSON NATIONAL 5 ENGLISH 2013

READING FOR UNDERSTANDING, ANALYSIS AND EVALUATION

1. Candidates should show they understand the meaning of the phrase by referring to examples which illustrate the idea.

   Any three from:

   - She gives examples/mentions specific famous people whom we think we know well
   - She uses "assume" to continue the idea of "illusion"
   - She uses "familiar" to continue the idea of "intimacy"
   - She uses "know everything there is to know" to continue the idea of "intimacy"
   - We think we know all about what David Beckham wears
   - We feel we know personal details about Prince William
   - We know all about how and when JK Rowling wrote her books/we know as much about JK Rowling's method of writing as we do about her.

2. Candidates should demonstrate their understanding of the similarities between JK Rowling's life/experiences and Cinderella's life/experiences.

   Any four ideas from:

   - Both "endured" cold living conditions
   - Both were on their own/single
   - Both were poor
   - Both had their lives altered for the better
   - Both found husbands.

3. Candidates should explain how the word choice shows the negative effects of fame.

   Any two from:

   - "begging letters" – implies unpleasant/unwanted attention
   - Journalists "rifling" through her bins – suggests invasion of privacy/indiscriminate searching and/or unpleasant/unwanted attention
   - Photographers "lurking" on the beach – implies covert/hidden/suspicion/being observed from a distance and/or unpleasant/unwanted attention
   - "Strangers" implies people she does not know giving her unwanted attention
   - "Accosted" implies unwanted attention/a sense of danger
   - "In the supermarket" implies she cannot perform everyday tasks.

4. Candidates should identify the advantages and disadvantages of fame as expressed by JK Rowling.

   Each advantage or disadvantage supported by detailed comment can be awarded a maximum of two marks.

Advantages:
- A sense of validation. "I don't feel like quite such a waste of space anymore."
- Implied relationship with her fans.

Disadvantages:
- She feels guilty about her wealth
- Fears life after Harry – she is worried about being taken seriously as an adult writer/that she will not be able to move on
- She feels she will only be known for writing about Harry Potter.

5. Candidates should identify a rhetorical question and discuss its effect.

   Any one question identified plus one explanation from:

   - "William, of course, has nothing to sell – or has he?" Plus effect of the question which is to question the marketability of Prince William's qualities.
   - "Is he willing to surrender the chance of a relatively normal life to be the modern face of monarchy?" Plus effect of the question which is to emphasise the dilemma Prince William faces.

6. Candidates should demonstrate understanding of the ways in which JK Rowling feels she is "fortunate" by giving evidence from the text.

   Any four ideas from:

   - Her fame is not based on who she is
   - Her fame is not based on what she looks like
   - Her fame is not based on her family connections
   - She is famous for her imagination/writing/characters
   - People discuss her work and not her
   - Paraphrased version of "we know Harry, and his magic is likely to last."

7. Candidates should infer the writer's attitude to JK Rowling and support this with evidence from the text.

   One mark for identifying the attitude and one mark for relevant quotation.

   Writer's attitude – positive, admiring. Plus at least one piece of evidence from the following list:

   - "reassure"
   - "success"
   - "her own invention"
   - "millions"
   - "his magic is likely to last"

8. Candidates should choose one of the images and analyse its effect.

   For three marks, candidates should state the comparison and show how it is linked to the example used in the passage. This would be considered a full analysis.

   Freeze-frame = a still from a moving image/photograph

   Logo = brand name

   Crashing edifice = a falling structure.

For example:

Fame is compared to a photograph which cannot be changed. This shows how difficult it would be for JK Rowling to change her career path.

9. Candidates should summarise the nature of fame, according to the writer.

    Any four points from:

    Key points:

    • We think we know famous people well

    • We are surprised to hear famous people in reality

    • Advantages of fame (could be several)

    • Disadvantages of fame (could be several)

    • Reasons for fame, eg personality, skill, family.

NATIONAL 5 ENGLISH
SPECIMEN QUESTION PAPER

CRITICAL READING

SECTION 1. Critical Essay

Categories are not grades. The five categories are designed primarily to assist with placing each candidate response at an appropriate point on a continuum of achievement.

	20-18 Category 1	17-14 Category 2	13-10 Category 3	9-5 Category 4	4-0 Category 5
The candidate demonstrates:	• **a high degree of familiarity** with the text as a whole • **very good understanding** of the central concerns of the text • a line of thought which is **consistently relevant** to the task	• **familiarity** with the text as a whole • **good understanding** of the central concerns of the text • a line of thought which is **relevant** to the task, although there may be some disproportion in parts of the essay	• **generally sound familiarity** with the text as a whole • **some understanding** of the central concerns of the text • a line of thought which is **mostly relevant** to the task	• **some familiarity with some aspects** of the text • **attempts** a line of thought **but this is not always maintained**	Although such essays should be rare, in this category, the candidate's essay will demonstrate one or more of the following: • it contains numerous errors in spelling/grammar/ punctuation/ sentence construction/ paragraphing • knowledge and understanding of the text(s) are not used to answer the question • any analysis and evaluation attempted are unconvincing • the answer is simply too thin
Analysis of the text demonstrates:	• **thorough awareness** of the writer's techniques through analysis, making **confident** use of critical terminology • **very detailed/thoughtful** explanation of stylistic devices supported by a **range of well-chosen** references and/or quotations	• **sound awareness** of the writer's techniques through analysis, making **good use** of critical terminology • **detailed** explanation of stylistic devices supported by **appropriate** reference and/or quotation	• **an awareness** of the writer's techniques through analysis, making **some use** of critical terminology • explanation of stylistic devices supported by **some appropriate** reference and/ or quotation	• **some awareness of the more obvious** techniques used by the writer through **explanation** • **attempts to use** critical terminology • **description** of **some** stylistic devices followed by some reference and/or quotation	
Evaluation of the text is shown through:	• **a very well developed** commentary of what has been enjoyed/gained from the text(s), supported by **a range of** well-chosen references to its **relevant** features	• **a well developed** commentary of what has been enjoyed/gained from the text(s), supported by **appropriate** reference to its **relevant** features	• **generally sound** commentary of what has been enjoyed/gained from the text(s), supported by **some appropriate** reference to its features	• **brief** commentary of what has been enjoyed/gained from the text(s), followed by **brief** reference to its features	
The candidate	• uses language to communicate a line of thought **very clearly** • uses spelling, grammar, sentence construction and punctuation which are consistently accurate • structures the essay **effectively to enhance** meaning/purpose • uses paragraphing which is **accurate and effective**	• uses language to communicate a line of thought **clearly** • uses spelling, grammar, sentence construction and punctuation which are **sufficiently** accurate • structures the essay **very well** • uses paragraphing which is **accurate**	• uses language to communicate a line of thought **at first reading** • uses spelling, grammar, sentence construction and punctuation which are **mainly accurate** • attempts to structure the essay **in an appropriate way** • uses paragraphing which is **mainly accurate**	• uses language to communicate a line of thought which may be disorganised and/or difficult to follow • makes some errors in spelling/ grammar/punctuation/ sentence construction • has not structured the essay well • has made some errors in paragraphing	
In summary, the candidate's essay is	thorough and precise (Very good)	very detailed and shows some insight (Good)	fairly detailed and relevant (Satisfactory)	lacks detail and relevance (Approaching satisfactory)	superficial and/or technically weak (Significant flaws)

SECTION 2 - Scottish Text

SCOTTISH TEXT (DRAMA)

Question 1—The Steamie by Tony Roper

1. Any four aspects of women's lives at that time for one mark each.

    Possible answers include:
    *   Rise early in the morning
    *   Relentless cleaning/washing/food preparation
    *   Looking after children
    *   Looking after husband
    *   Lack of money
    *   Having to work as well as having all the household responsibilities
    *   Considered by society at the time to be inferior to men
    *   Lack of free/leisure/personal time
    *   No time to eat lunch
    *   Trying to keep children happy
    *   Doing housework until late at night
    *   Lack of husband's support.

2. Candidates should show how the word choice used shows how women's efforts are not appreciated.

    Possible answers include:
    *   "(unpaid) skivvies" suggests they are seen as servants
    *   "used" suggests their families see them only for what they can get from them
    *   "mince is lumpy" or "chips too warm" suggests the family complain about the quality of the meals
    *   "ain wee job" suggests their paid employment is not considered important.

3. (a) Three marks can be awarded for one/two quotations and very detailed comment(s) or three quotations with more straightforward comments.

    Magrit's feelings towards her children are mostly warm, loving, affectionate, caring, etc.

    One mark should be given for identifying a suitable feeling.

    Candidates might refer to:
    *   "get the weans ready and oot the hoose lookin' as tidy and as well dressed as ye can afford" shows her desire for them to be well presented/give them the best she can
    *   "run home, cooked something for the weans" shows she puts herself out/makes a big effort to feed them at lunchtime
    *   "even if I am being used . . . I don't mind" shows she doesn't care that her efforts go unacknowledged
    *   "I love my family" shows in plain language her devotion to her children
    *   "any minute noo the weans'll be in" shows she is looking forward to seeing the children
    *   "the weans arrive and ye gie them shortbread, sultana cake, ginger wine" shows she is generous towards them

    *   There is also a suggestion that she is slightly irritated by their inability to suggest something to eat and claim they will eat "anything" when they decline everything she suggests.

    (b) Three marks can be awarded for one/two quotations and very detailed comment(s) or three quotations with more straightforward comments.

    Magrit's feelings towards her husband include contempt, disappointment, irritation, etc. This is mainly revealed through comments which could be seen as genuine but are in fact sarcastic/ironic.

    One mark should be given for identifying a suitable feeling.

    Candidates might refer to:
    *   "the lord high provider" shows the high status her husband/society expects with which she clearly doesn't agree
    *   "get him oot" shows she is keen for him to leave quickly so she can get on with other things
    *   Any part of "the men tae have a drink, cause they need wan . . . the souls . . . efter pittin' in a hard day's graft" shows that she doesn't agree that men's lives are as difficult as they think they are OR are not as difficult as women's lives
    *   "there is just one thing missin'" shows that he is not always around for family occasions
    *   "the head of the family" is clearly sarcastic as he doesn't appear to contribute anything to the home other than financially
    *   "ready to make the evening complete" is clearly sarcastic as he is likely to ruin the evening/or provide an appropriate finish to a day which has already been very difficult or tiring
    *   "what is staunin there" shows she does not refer to him as "who" suggesting there is something less than human about her husband
    *   "your better half" is clearly sarcastic as she does not believe that he is superior to her
    *   "the man who was goin' to make you the happiest woman in the world" shows that her marriage has not lived up to her expectations
    *   "that. (At ANDY.)" By comparing him to Andy (who is drunk at this point in the play) shows that her husband is drunk and she will need to look after him.

4. Candidates should identify features/roles of men and women's lives at the time with reference to the text in the form of quotations and/or examples to support the points being made. It may be that a candidate will identify more points in relation to women and should still be rewarded as appropriate. For example, a candidate who identifies four aspects for women and only three for men may still score eight marks.

    Candidates who only deal with one gender (most likely women) are limited to half marks, although understanding or awareness of men's roles may be implicit in these answers and may gain some credit.

8-7 marks

Candidates should identify and comment on three or four aspects of gender as demonstrated in the play with quotations and/or specific examples to support their answer.

- Skilled discussion of three or four aspects of both genders
- Still skilled but lacking some assurance.

6-5 marks

Candidates should identify and comment on two or three aspects of gender as demonstrated in the play with quotations and/or specific examples to support their answer.

- Confident discussion of two or three aspects per gender
- Slightly less confident discussion of two or three aspects per gender.

4-3 marks

Candidates should identify and comment on one or two aspects of gender as demonstrated in the play with quotations and/or specific examples to support their answer.

- Discussion of one or two roles per gender
- Weaker discussion of one or two roles per gender.

2-1 marks

There should be a generalised acknowledgement of male and female roles at the time, with some generalised reference to the text.

- Generalised identification of one role per gender with generalised reference to the play in support of this
- Generalised identification of one role (for either gender).

SCOTTISH TEXT (PROSE)

Question 2—*Treasure Island* by Robert Louis Stevenson

1. Three points to be made.
   One mark for each point.

   Possible answers include:

   - man comes to inn;
   - man checks location;
   - man asks to be taken to captain;
   - Jim gives warning against seeing captain;
   - man (forcibly) insists;
   - captain shocked to see man;
   - man gives captain something (the black spot);
   - man leaves;
   - captain reacts with initial defiance;
   - captain collapses/dies.

2. Statement of acceptable mood or atmosphere for one mark.
   Example of use of writer's use of language for one mark.
   Comment for one mark.

   Possible answers include:

   Mood or atmosphere:

   - Gloomy, sad, depressing, mysterious, etc.

Writer's use of language:

- "funeral" — sad time
- "bitter" — cold (literally or metaphorically)/ unpleasant/uncomfortable
- "foggy" — gloomy/dark
- "frosty" — cold/uncomfortable
- "deformed" — unpleasant
- "dreadful" — frightening/unpleasant
- "hood" — mysterious

3. Marks can be awarded for two examples with detailed comments or three/four examples with less detailed comments.

   Possible answers include:

   Word choice:

   - "horrible" — threatening
   - "creature" — non-human, alarming

   Metaphor:

   - "gripped... like a vice" — aggressive/controlling

   Use of imperative:

   - "Now boy...take me to the captain"
   - "Take me in straight or I'll break your arm"
   - "Come now march"
   - All commands are aggressive/threatening

   Word choice:

   - "sneered" — dismissive
   - "(made me) cry out" — sense of pain/harm
   - "cruel" "cold" "ugly" — all have connotations of threat
   - "it cowed me" — he is made to feel small/frightened
   - "(holding me in) an iron fist" — real threat/control.

4. There should be some understanding of the contrast between the beggar's previous movements and those after he completes his errand.

   The beggar has moved so freely and easily considering how infirm he had seemed.

5. Candidates should show understanding of how the character of Jim changes and develops as the story progresses.

   There should be at least one detailed reference to an aspect of Jim's character as it is revealed to the reader in this extract, and then detailed reference made to two other incidents from other points in the narrative.

   8-7 marks

   Candidates should make detailed reference to an aspect of Jim's character from this extract plus comment.

   Candidates should make detailed reference to aspects of Jim's character from two other points in the narrative.

   - Skillful discussion of above
   - Skill shown, but lacks assurance.

   6-5 marks

   Candidates should make detailed reference to aspect of Jim's character from this extract plus comment.

   Candidates should make detailed reference to Jim's character from two other points in the narrative.

   - Reasonably confident discussion of the above
   - Less confident discussion of the above.

4-3 marks

Candidates should make reasonably detailed reference to aspect of Jim's character from this extract.

Candidates should make reasonably detailed reference to Jim's character from at least one other point in the narrative.

- Some discussion and detail of the above attempted
- Some (but incomplete) discussion of the above.

2-1 marks

Candidates should make reference to one aspect of Jim's character from this extract.

Candidates should make one reference to Jim's character from one other point in narrative.

- Two references with attempt to provide detail
- One reference with attempt to provide detail.

SCOTTISH TEXT (POETRY)

Question 3 — *Composed in August* by Robert Burns

1. (a) Two marks can be awarded for two main ideas or concerns shown in stanza one.
   - Man is destructive/violent/aggressive (towards animals/nature)
   - Autumn is a relaxing/peaceful/soothing season
   - Nature is plentiful/attractive/soothing
   - Love/thoughts of love gives pleasure
   - People are different (some fire guns, some walk alone, some are active, some are thoughtful).

   (b) Four marks can be awarded for two examples of language helping to clarify or illustrate meaning.
   - Juxtaposition/contrast of "slaught'ring guns" with "(Autumn's) pleasant weather" makes clear his point about man's capacity for violence/destruction
   - Word choice of "springs" makes clear creatures' fear of man
   - Alliteration in "westlin winds" emphasises his point about the soothing quality of nature
   - Alliteration in "waving grain, wide o'er the plain" emphasises how bountiful nature can be for the farmer
   - Rhyme of "bright" and "night" emphasises the poet's pleasure in walking/thinking of his love
   - Alliteration contained in "moon" and "muse" emphasises poet's pleasure in evening walk/thinking of his love
   - Word choice of "charmer" suggests poet is under love's spell.

2. Four marks can be awarded for showing how any **two** examples of the poet's use of language in stanza two or stanza three effectively contribute to the main ideas or concerns of the poem.
   - Repetition/list of different birds and their habitats shows how nature accommodates every creature
   - Repetition of word "loves" suggests birds' ease/at-homeness in their environment
   - Word choice of "shun" suggests man's rejection of/hostility to nature

- Use of rhyme in stanza two suggests unity/harmony in nature
- Use of contrast in stanza three suggests idea that the world/nature contains contrasting/conflicting elements
- Use of exclamations in stanza three indicates poet's anger at man's tyranny
- Word choice of "cruel"/"Tyrannic"/"gory" emphasises man's aggression/violence/destructive tendencies
- Juxtaposition of "sportsman's joy" with "murd'ring cry" suggests man's cruelty.

3. Candidates should show understanding of the term "conclusion" and show how the content of the last two stanzas continues ideas and/or language from the first three stanzas. Other examples are acceptable.
   - "Peggy (dear)" names the "charmer" mentioned in stanza one
   - Reference to evening ("the evening's clear") reprises reference to night in stanza one
   - "(skimming) swallow" refers back to mention of birds at start of poem
   - Reference to fields as "All fading-green and yellow" repeats earlier idea of nature's beauty
   - "Come let us stray our gladsome way" refers back to reference to pleasures of evening walking from stanza one
   - Listing of "rustling corn, the fruited thorn, /And ev'ry happy creature" repeats earlier idea of nature's bounty/place in nature for everything
   - References to love in final stanza reprise mentions of love in stanza one
   - References to farmer/harvest, etc in final stanza reprise idea of nature's bounty for farmer in stanza one.

4. Candidates should show awareness of the ideas and/or language of the wider works of Burns, and be able to relate this awareness to *Song Composed in August*.

   8-7 marks

   Candidates should identify at least three features/ideas in the poem and be able to comment on these in at least two other poems. The discussion should be supported by detailed quotation from the poems being discussed.
   - Skilled discussion of other Burns' poetry in relation to *Song Composed in August*
   - Still skilled, but lacking some assurance.

   6-5 marks

   Candidates should identify at least two features of ideas and/or language in the poem and be able to comment on these in at least two other poems. The discussion should be supported by several quotations from the poems being discussed.
   - Confident discussion of other Burns' poetry in relation to *Song Composed in August*
   - Slightly less confident discussion.

   4-3 marks

   Candidates should identify two features of ideas and/or language common to other poems. There should be at least two quotations from the poems to support the candidate's discussion.
   - Some discussion attempted of other Burns' poetry in relation to *Song Composed in August*
   - Weaker discussion.

2–1 marks

Candidates should identify at least one feature of ideas and/or language of other Burns' poetry in relation to *Song Composed in August* with at least one quotation.

Acknowledgement of common feature(s) with general reference.

NATIONAL 5 ENGLISH
MODEL PAPER 1

Reading for Understanding, Analysis and Evaluation

1. Any four of the following for one mark each:
   - tennis players are very superstitious
   - they believe that certain behaviour can affect results
   - research was carried out on pigeons
   - it was discovered that they could be made to believe that certain actions …
   - … caused certain outcomes …
   - … even though there was no connection.

2. (a) Any two of the following for one mark each:
     - he believes in the power of superstition
     - he is irrational
     - he is unshakeable/dogmatic
     - he is unaware of his irrational stance.

   (b) Reference to/explanation of any two of the following for one mark each:
     - use of "even"
     - as a cricketer, he is thought to be more intelligent than other sportspeople
     - use of "even though"
     - "threadbare and smelly" – not what we would expect of a professional sportsman
     - prepared to inconvenience team-mates.

3. Any four of the following for one mark each:
   - a superstition can be based on a false belief …
   - … and therefore can lead to unnecessary behaviour
   - but mostly this causes no damage …
   - … provided observing it does not cause huge inconvenience
   - a superstition can be based on a genuine danger/fear …
   - … in which case observing it is beneficial.

4. Key features (any two from):
   - repeated/parallel structure, consisting of
   - "some believe/like …"
   - followed by comma
   - followed by "but"
   - semicolons create list.

   Conveys point by (any two from):
   - illustrating just how many different ways people don't let superstition influence them too much
   - showing how similar all these beliefs are
   - showing how easy it is to find examples.

5. (a) It can be seen as either effective or not effective:

effective because	just as a spectrum contains a whole range/ variety/scale (of colours)	so there is a (wide) range of superstitions/ (illogical) behaviours/ perceptions/beliefs
not effective because	the (bright) colour imagery implied	is not apt or fitting or helpful to describe/illustrate the (melancholy) subject

(b) Any of the following:

- it illustrates his point about the range of "irrationality" by providing an extreme example of superstition

- it illustrates his point that superstition taken to excess/dogmatically insisted upon has an unhelpful/deleterious effect/outcome

- he is using reference to a team game to show the influence of superstition on others.

(c) Any of the following:

- the reference to the elements of help and hindrance recaps the idea of ambivalence explored elsewhere in the passage

- (metaphor) "kick (the ritual into touch)" reprises references to football/sport used earlier

- "With a rabbit's foot, obviously" reprises the cynical/sceptical/ humorous tone seen elsewhere

6. Any two of the following for two marks each:

- "funny bunch" — slang, off-hand way to describe sportspeople

- "bring the world collapsing" — exaggeration

- "poor dears" — mock concern

- "Yes, really" — suddenly as if speaking directly to reader

- "feathered fellows" — as if they're human

- "I know, I know" — pretending to be hearing readers' derision

- "(pigeons) unavailable for interview" — as if they're human, mocking the standard official response to a difficult question

- "got up the noses" — slang (+ playful mixing of literal and metaphorical)

- "abode" — deliberately exaggerated way to describe a cave

- "scarpers"— (old fashioned) slang sounds out of place for such a threat

- "his five-a-day" — anachronistic reference to modern nutritional theory.

7. Any four of the following for one mark each (may be in bullet point form or in prose):

- superstitions can been observed in eminent sportspeople

- pigeons can be trained to act as if superstitious

- superstition arises when there is a belief that one action can lead directly to another ...

- ... even when no connection exists

- some/most superstitions are harmless ...

- ... and observing them can bring comfort/hope/peace of mind

- some superstitions lead to damaging behaviour.

NATIONAL 5 ENGLISH
MODEL PAPER 1

Critical Reading

SECTION 1 — Critical Essay

Please see the assessment criteria for the Critical Essay on pages 84 to 85.

SECTION 2 — Scottish Context

SCOTTISH TEXT (DRAMA)

Sailmaker by Alan Spence

1. Any four valid points. Possible answers include:
   - he is not earning a lot from his job
   - he is gambling heavily
   - he has suffered a significant loss (backing a favourite)
   - he is in debt to the bookie
   - he is paying high interest/not paying off original sum.

2. Any one valid character point and textual support. Possible answers include:
   - generous – extends loan
   - caring – wants to know what the problem is
   - knows his brother well – suspects drink/knows it's not just the job
   - persistent – doesn't let Davie fob him off
   - nosey/intrusive – keeps asking questions about brother's private life.

3. One or more of the following. Simple point and more developed explanation required. Possible answers include:
   - he knows his brother is (sort of) joking
   - he realises brother is trying to relieve some tension
   - he is amused at the fact brother can bring his sectarianism into anything
   - he realises that the bookie's religion is not going to change anything.

4. The key point is the contrast between Davie's steadfast optimism and Billy's realistic/cynical view of life; identifying this and making reference to at least two different parts of the exchange should gain four marks.

   Reference could be made to several occasions when a hopeful comment by Davie is countered by a pessimistic/realistic putdown from his brother, eg:
   - the scathing "Whatever that is" showing that Billy lacks Davie's faith
   - the blunt assertions "It's a mug's game. The punter canny win" in response to Davie's rather feeble "Things've got tae get better."
   - the frustrated "Flingin it away!" in response to Davie's dogged "Got tae keep trying."
   - a further contrast can be identified in lines 42-49 where Billy's desire for positive action is met with Davie's passivity ("Ah knew his terms") , culminating in his shoulder-shrugging "Whit a carry on, eh?".

5. Answers should deal with a number of relevant aspects of how money problems and escape are explored in the play, e.g.
   - Davie's gambling
   - Davie's drinking
   - Billy's move to Aberdeen for work
   - exchanges between Alec and Ian about work prospects
   - the idea of education as a way to betterment
   - football (and sectarianism) as a diversion from poverty
   - religion as an "escape"
   - specific details of Davie's and Alec's situation.

   Marks are allocated as follows:

   8-7 marks
   identify and comment on three or four aspects of the theme as demonstrated in the play with quotations and/or specific examples to support the answer.

   6-5 marks
   identify and comment on two or three aspects of the theme as demonstrated in the play with quotations and/or specific examples to support the answer.

   4-3 marks
   identify and comment on one or two aspects of the theme as demonstrated in the play with quotations and/or specific examples to support the answer.

   2-1 marks
   a generalised acknowledgement of the theme, with some generalised reference to the text.

SCOTTISH TEXT (PROSE)

The Cone Gatherers by Robin Jenkins

1. Any four valid points. Possible answers include:
   - Duror is unable to climb tree
   - Neil is initially polite
   - Duror delivers message to Calum and Neil about the deer drive
   - Neil protests strongly
   - the effect on Duror of being unable to climb the tree is evident.

2. Two brief points for 1 mark each, or a good overall response (e.g. on sound) for 2 marks. Possible answers include:
   - the use of a series of rather threatening sounds — "scrapes", "thumps", "cracked", "barked"
   - the frequency of short sentences — creates a breathless, staccato effect
   - the alternation between sound and silence — creates suspense
   - the references to waiting, once for "three or four minutes" – an agonisingly long time.

3. There should be reference to at least three of the following in order to establish two changes, with each attitude supported by some valid reference to the text:
   - friendly/polite (line16)
   - helpful (line 19)

- hopeful/anticipating good news (lines 23 and 25)
- non-committal/defensive (line 27)
- angry/slightly aggressive (lines 30-31)
- disbelieving/indignant (lines 33-35)
- very assertive (lines 35-37).

4. Clear explanation for two marks and one mark for a less confident explanation. A possible answer is:
   - on the outside he appears normal/healthy, but a malignant force is destroying him from within.

5. Answers should show a good knowledge of what happens at the deer drive and of the significance it has for the novel as a whole. Reference could be made to:
   - Calum's revulsion/desire to protect nature and wildlife
   - Duror's bizarre behaviour
   - Lady Runcie-Campbell's reaction
   - the incident as a turning point in the conflict between Duror and the Cone-Gatherers.

   Marks are allocated as follows:

   8-7 marks
   identify and comment on three or four ways in which the deer drive is important in developing character or theme, using specific references to support the answer.

   6-5 marks
   identify and comment on two or three ways in which the deer drive is important in developing character or theme, using specific references to support the answer.

   4-3 marks
   identify and comment on one or two ways in which the deer drive is important in developing character or theme, using specific references to support the answer.

   2-1 marks
   a generalised acknowledgement of the importance of the deer drive, with some generalised reference to the text.

SCOTTISH TEXT (PROSE)

Short Stories by Anne Donovan

1. Any four valid points. Possible answers include:
   - "shimmerin wi light" — alluring, attractive, etc
   - "brightness sharp against the gloomy street" — contrast to emphasise the appeal of the square
   - "like the plastic jewellery sets wee lassies love" — connotations of precious jewels, bright and shiny, children's enjoyment of play
   - "in a mad rhythm" — uncontrolled, zany, exhilarating, etc
   - "ae their ain" — idea of freedom, lack of constraint, etc
   - "bells ringin and snow fallin" — association with Christmas fun (+ rhythmical pattern to heighten the sense of involvement)
   - "Reindeer and Santas, holly, ivy, robins …" — list to emphasise to the sheer number of attractions
   - "bleezin wi light" — as if on fire, extraordinarily bright, etc
   - "fillin the air" — the sound is pervasive, dominates the senses

- "like a cracklin heavenly choir" — as if angels are present; suggestions of warmth, comfort, etc.

2. A well-made point for two marks and a less assured response for one mark. Possible answers include:
   - to convey the excitement of others around them
   - to give the impression of a babble of disembodied voices everywhere
   - to give a rapid glimpse of some of the attractions (reindeer, star, tree).

3. Possible answers include:
   - in the past people on the benches were easily identified as down-and-outs
   - today they looked no different from ordinary shoppers.

4. Four brief, valid points for one mark each. Possible answers include:
   - Amy tugging at mother's arm to attract attention
   - Sandra's "Whit song?" as if she's not been paying attention
   - Sandra's "Do you?" as if struggling to show some interest
   - Amy's gushing detail about school and Mrs Anderson
   - Sandra's very uninterested "Oh."
   - Sandra's "What's no your favourite?" — she hasn't been paying attention at all
   - Amy initiates guessing game
   - Sandra won't play along ("Don't know.")
   - Amy's wheedling "Guess, Mammy, you have tae guess."
   - Sandra joins in to keep the peace (because she knows that's how to get it over with)
   - Amy quickly resorts to "Gie in?"
   - Sandra accepts with alacrity
   - Amy's triumphant "Ah've won!" …
   - … followed almost without a break by a question demanding an explanation.

5. Answers should show a detailed knowledge of the chosen story and focus on the development of the parent/child relationship within it. Of the stories on the set list, the most profitable will be: "All That Glisters" or "Dear Santa" or, to a lesser degree, "Virtual Pals". It is acceptable in this question to write about a short story by Anne Donovan which is not on the set list.

   Marks are allocated as follows:

   8-7 marks
   identify and comment on three or four aspects of the parent/child relationship as explored in the chosen story with quotations and/or specific reference to support the answer.

   6-5 marks
   identify and comment on two or three aspects of the parent/child relationship as explored in the chosen story with quotations and/or specific reference to support the answer.

   4-3 marks
   identify and comment on one or two aspects of the parent/child relationship as explored in the chosen story with quotations and/or specific reference to support the answer.

2-1 marks

a generalised acknowledgement of the parent/child relationship in the chosen story, with some generalised reference to the text.

SCOTTISH TEXT (POETRY)

Poems by Carol Ann Duffy

1. Four brief, valid points for one mark each. Possible answers include:

   - "a spinning world" — suggests speed, exhilaration, etc
   - "castles" — suggests fairy-tale romance, luxury, security, etc
   - "torchlight" — suggests carnival atmosphere, brightness, etc
   - "clifftops" — suggests dizzy height, dominance, distant horizons, etc
   - "forests, castles, torchlight, clifftops, seas" — list suggests profusion of exciting features
   - "dive for pearls" — suggests romantic, exotic, etc
   - "shooting stars" — suggests brightness, speed, exhilaration, etc
   - "kisses/on these lips" — tactile, sensual, etc.

2. For each reference, two marks for a detailed comment and one mark for a more basic comment. (No marks simply for selecting a word/expression.)

   Reference could be made to any of the following. **NB:** The comments given below are suggestions only; there will be other, perfectly acceptable, interpretations.

   - "rhyme" — suggesting the lovers' connectedness, sense of belonging together, fulfilling each other
   - "assonance" — suggesting they are similar, connected, but retaining some individuality
   - "verb dancing in the centre of a noun" — suggesting her lover's ability to bring life, movement, action … this is a complex image which allows many analyses
   - "he'd written me" — as if she is his creation, she owes everything to him
   - "a page beneath his writer's hands" — presents her as a passive recipient of his creativity
   - "drama (played)" — as if the senses referred to are actors in some greater performance.

3. (a) Brief comment on both of the following for one mark each or detailed comment on either for two marks:

   - "dozed" — sleeping (with a suggestion of indolence), while the others are more energetically and pleasurably engaged
   - "dribbling" — connotations of old age and messiness compared with the others' apparent vitality and clarity of purpose
   - "prose" — suggests their lives are dull, ordinary, uninspired, unlike the imaginative "poetry" of the others' love-making.

   (b) Acceptable comment and valid reference for two marks. Possible answers include:

   - fondness
   - respect
   - sadness at his death
   - devotion

4. Answers should show a detailed knowledge of the chosen poem and focus on the development of the theme of love within it. Of the poems on the set list, the most profitable will be: "Valentine" or "Havisham" or, to a lesser degree "Mrs Midas". It is acceptable in this question to write about a poem by Carol Ann Duffy which is not on the set list.

   Marks are allocated as follows:

   8-7 marks

   identify and comment on three or four aspects of the way love is explored in the chosen poem with quotations and/or specific reference to support the answer.

   6-5 marks

   identify and comment on two or three aspects of the way love is explored in the chosen poem with quotations and/or specific reference to support the answer.

   4-3 marks

   identify and comment on one or two aspects of the way love is explored in the chosen poem with quotations and/or specific reference to support the answer.

   2-1 marks

   a generalised acknowledgement of the theme of love in the chosen poem, with some generalised reference to the text.

NATIONAL 5 ENGLISH
MODEL PAPER 2

Reading for Understanding, Analysis and Evaluation

1. One mark for selection and one mark for comment. Any two from:
   - "wrecking" — suggests destruction, violence, etc
   - "vandals" — suggests mindless destruction, etc
   - "Genghis Khan" — associated with uncivilised behaviour, etc
   - "destroying" — suggests demolishing, tearing down, etc
   - "pillaging" — suggests looting, stealing, etc
   - alliteration ("pillaging out punctuation") — adds some weight to the criticism
   - "savaging" — suggests viciously tearing apart, etc
   - alliteration ("savaging our sentences") — adds some weight to the criticism
   - "textese" — suffix "-ese" is pejorative
   - "slanguage" — combines 'language' with 'slang', which is looked down on
   - "virus" — suggests disease, something harmful, etc
   - "bleak" — suggests poverty of language
   - "bald" — suggests plainness of language
   - "shorthand" — suggests superficial, etc
   - "drab" — suggests dreariness, monotony, etc
   - "masks" — suggests concealment, deceit, etc.

2. (a) • reaction to texting has been both positive and negative
       • reaction to others was negative.

   (b) One mark for selection of feature and one mark for comment.
       - use of "ever" ("has there ever been") — suggests he thinks it could be unique
       - list of reactions — shows just how wide-ranging they are
       - use of (rhetorical) question — to make reader think it must be something remarkable.

3. Any three of the following for one mark each:
   - people think it's something entirely new, but it's not
   - people think it's only young people who use it, but it's not
   - people think it impedes reading and writing, but (possibly) it actually improves it
   - people think it will cause lasting harm, but its effect will be slight/short-lived.

4. One mark for selection of word and one mark for comment. Any two of the following:
   - "hysteria" — suggests critics are in panic, raising irrational objections, etc
   - "swallowed whole" — suggests critics' gullibility, etc
   - "stories"/"reports" — suggests critics are prepared to believe unverified accounts

   - "incessantly" — suggests critics are obsessive, won't stop to consider other arguments
   - "hoax" — suggests critics are prepared to believe something made up.

5. Reference to and/or explanation of the significance of any three of the following for one mark each:
   - historical pedigree (for use of initials)
   - "English literary tradition" — sounds dignified, academic, established, accepted as being of value, etc
   - reference to OED — the most respected dictionary, hallmark of quality, etc
   - reference to four highly respected writers.

6. One mark for each of the following explanations:
   - line 55: precedes/introduces an expansion/explanation of the "extraordinary number of ways ..."
   - line 57: precedes/introduces an expansion/explanation of what "Professional writers" do
   - line 60: creates pause before adding the most the contentious aspect, the one about which critics blame texting most.

7. One mark for selection of word or feature and one for comment. Any two of the following:
   - two similar sentences at start — suggests a balance, calmness, nothing to get worked up about
   - "merely" — minimises any negative effect
   - "creative" — suggests something imaginative, positive, worthy, etc
   - "suit the demands" — suggests something helpful, co-operative, etc
   - "no ... not ... not" — repetition assures us all the bad things will not happen
   - "evolution" — suggests growth, improvement, etc.

8. Any five of the following for one mark each (may be in bullet point form or in prose):
   - features criticised in texting have a long historical pedigree
   - text language is an understandable response to the design of the keypad
   - text language is an understandable way to save time
   - abbreviations are common elsewhere
   - people, especially children, enjoy playing with language
   - playing with language helps develop linguistic skills
   - texters are already skilled in the use of language
   - there is no correct form of English (from which texters are deviating).

Critical Reading

SECTION 1 — Critical Essay

Please see the assessment criteria for the Critical Essay on pages 84 to 85.

SECTION 2 — Scottish Context

SCOTTISH TEXT (DRAMA)

Tally's Blood by Ann Marie di Mambro

1. (a) One mark for acceptable aspect of character and one mark for valid textual reference. Possible answers include:

    - self-centred — ignores Lucia's attempts to speak

    - snobbish/class-conscious — looks up/wants to impress to Palombos; looks down on others (the type who boast "Ma lassie cleaned four chickens.")

    - traditional — determined to marry Lucia to an Italian

    - ambitious for Lucia — wants to marry her into a "good" family

    - fantasist/delusional — convinced Lucia is "daft for" Silvio Palombo.

    (b) Either of the following:

    - her repeated "He's okay" — polite but very committal/no enthusiasm at all

    - the repeated "Auntie Rosinella ...?" interrogative tone, trying to change the subject (to her wish to attend the wedding).

2. Any three of the following for two marks each:

    - she maintains that Italian men work harder than others — but the audience can actually see Hughie working hard ("like a Trojan")

    - she maintains that "Nobody loves their families like the Italians" — but immediately after that Hughie declines to stay for some food, because of a duty he feels to his mother

    - she displays obvious distaste for extra-marital sex (seen as a typical fault of Scottish people), when the audience is in no doubt about what happened between Franco and Bridget

    - she is contemptuous of Scottish men's propensity for alcohol ("Give him two or three days ...") — but within seconds we see Hughie declining the offer of a drink from Massimo.

3. Answers should show detailed knowledge of Rosinella's character throughout the play; how her prejudices are made known to the audience, and how by the end these have been erased. Reference to Act Two Scenes 10-14 will be of considerable importance to show how her view of Italian men and their qualities is changed by comparing the reality with her idealised/romanticised version in Glasgow.

Marks are allocated as follows:

8-7 marks
identify and comment on three or four aspects of Rosinella's prejudice as demonstrated in the play with quotations and/or specific examples to support the answer.

6-5 marks
identify and comment on two or three aspects of Rosinella's prejudice as demonstrated in the play with quotations and/or specific examples to support the answer.

4-3 marks
identify and comment on one or two aspects of Rosinella's prejudice as demonstrated in the play with quotations and/or specific examples to support the answer.

2-1 marks
a generalised acknowledgement of Rosinella's prejudice, with some generalised reference to the text.

SCOTTISH TEXT (PROSE)

Kidnapped by Robert Louis Stevenson

1. Three brief references and comment for one mark each. Possible answers include:

    - "steady"/"quiet"/"great stillness" — idea of unnerving peacefulness, calm before the storm, etc

    - "muttering voices" — can't be made out, so slightly threatening, etc

    - "clash of steel" — sudden sharp noise to break the silence, use of onomatopoeia

    - "dealing out the cutlasses" — disturbing idea of dangerous weapons being handed out, an idea of what David and Alan will have to face

    - return to "silence" — again nerve-racking, uneasy, etc.

2. Any two of the following for one mark each:

    - uncertainty

    - fear

    - hopelessness

    - anger

    - desire for it to be over.

3. Any three valid points with some textual support for one mark each. Possible answers include:

    - "all of a sudden" — surprise, frightening

    - "a rush of feet" — speed, threat, etc

    - "a roar" — aggressive sound

    - "and ... and ... and" — structure (list form) gives impression of one action following quickly after another

    - "someone crying out as if hurt" — uncertainty

    - "I cried" — the exclamation shows his state of alarm

    - "Look to your window!" — Alan's response draws attention to more danger

    - "pass his sword through the mate's body" — gruesome killing

    - "drive the door in" — idea of force, threat

- "But it was now or never" — idea of last chance, resolved to fate
- "shot into their midst" — reckless, desperate action
- "the whole party threw down the yard and ran for it" — sense of victory (albeit short-lived).

4. Any two valid points for one mark each. Possible answers include:

   - bloodthirsty ("his sword was running blood to the hilt")
   - proud ("himself so swelled with triumph")
   - impressive appearance ("looked to be invincible")
   - believer in cause ("There's one of your Whigs for ye!")
   - callous ("asked if I had done much execution").

5. What they've experienced so far is nothing much ("but a dram"); much worse, a more substantial battle is yet to come ("meat")

6. Answers should show an awareness of the changing relationship between David and Alan and refer appropriately to the text.

   Marks are allocated as follows:

   8-7 marks
   identify and comment on three or four aspects of the relationship between David and Alan and how it changes in the course of the novel, using specific references to support the answer.

   6-5 marks
   identify and comment on two or three aspects of the relationship between David and Alan and how it changes in the course of the novel, using specific references to support the answer.

   4-3 marks
   identify and comment on one or two aspects of the relationship between David and Alan and how it changes in the course of the novel, using specific references to support the answer.

   2-1 marks
   a generalised acknowledgement of the relationship between David and Alan and how it changes in the course of the novel, with some generalised reference to the text.

SCOTTISH TEXT (PROSE)

Short stories by Iain Crichton Smith

1. **Before** (any three of):
   - British officer (Colin Macleod) leaves the trenches
   - comes across a ruined church
   - meets a deserter who lives in the crypt
   - the deserter had been studying for the ministry
   - insists on delivering a sermon.

   After:
   - he shoots Colin

2. Two references and brief valid comments for one mark each. Possible answers include:
   - "forced" — under compulsion, against his will
   - "what they call" — implies he doesn't agree

- his outlook ("gaze") was different from the army's
- "despised" — looked down on with contempt
- "feared" — caused him alarm
- list of the men's shortcomings — emphasises how many there were
- "fornicated" — immoral behaviour
- "spat" — disgusting, unhealthy
- "filthily" — lack of hygiene, lack of self-respect.

3. Any one of the following for two marks:
   - contrasts the horrors of war with a friendly/sociable game of football
   - contrasts the horrors of war with the sociable activity of sharing photographs
   - contrasts civilised behaviour of German officer with the bombardment to follow
   - contrasts the banality of looking at watch with horrors to come.

4. Any four of the following for one mark each:
   - used to think God was on the side of the innocent, but no longer
   - believes God is "absent"
   - God has left him alone to suffer
   - God has left the world to suffer
   - God doesn't care
   - God has allowed mankind to engage in the destruction of war.

5. Answers should focus on a suitable story and discuss the impact/effectiveness of the ending in terms of the story as a whole. Of the stories on the set list, the most profitable will be: "The Telegram" or "The Painter" or, to a lesser degree, "The Red Door" or "The Crater". It is acceptable in this question to write about a short story by Crichton Smith which is not on the set list.

   Marks are allocated as follows:

   8-7 marks
   explore effectively and in detail the relationship between the ending of the chosen story and the story as a whole, using quotations and/or specific reference to support the answer.

   6-5 marks
   explore in some detail the relationship between the ending of the chosen story and the story as a whole, using quotations and/or specific reference to support the answer.

   4-3 marks
   explore at a basic level the relationship between the ending of the chosen story and the story as a whole, using quotations and/or specific reference to support the answer.

   2-1 marks
   a generalised acknowledgement of effectiveness of the ending of the chosen story, with some generalised reference to the text.

SCOTTISH TEXT (POETRY)

Poems by Norman MacCaig

1. Two references and appropriate comment for two marks each. Possible answers include:

   - "combs my nostrils" — sense of irritation

   - "bobbing along" — uneven movement

   - "green and yellow corridors" — association with sickness, nausea

   - "seems a corpse" — uncertain. disorientated

   - "vanishes" — sense of mystery

   - "I will not feel, I will not/feel, until/I have to" — jerky rhythm conveys tension, disorientation.

2. Any one of the following possible responses with appropriate support from text:

   - admiration of their calmness

   - respect for their ability to cope with death/suffering

   - appreciation of their bright, uncomplaining approach/attitude.

3. Clear identification of the imagery and suitable comment for two marks each:

   - "white cave of forgetfulness" — comparison of room to a "cave" conveys idea of seclusion, isolation from rest of world

   - "trembles on its stalk" — comparison of arm to "stalk" conveys its thinness, fragility

   - "a glass fang is fixed,/not guzzling but giving" — comparison of drip to a "fang" creates ghoulish/ slightly amusing idea of vampire in reverse

   - "the distance of pain" — suggests that pain can in some way be measured and that he is aware of how much she is suffering.

4. A sensible answer with valid comment for two marks; a less assured answer will be awarded one mark.

   There are many possible responses and each has to be judged on its merits. Better answers will explore the oxymoron of "fruitless fruits" and/or the futility of "books that will not be read" and/or the impact of "only". Some sense of the speaker's mood/feelings should be included.

5. Answers should focus on a suitable poem and the way strong emotion is presented and explored in it. Of the poems on the set list, the most profitable will be: "Aunt Julia" or "Memorial" or "Sounds of the Day" or, to a lesser degree, "Assisi". It is acceptable in this question to write about a poem by MacCaig which is not on the set list.

   Marks are allocated as follows:

   8-7 marks
   identify and comment on three or four aspects of the way strong emotions are presented/explored in the chosen poem with quotations and/or specific reference to support the answer.

   6-5 marks
   identify and comment on two or three aspects of the way strong emotions are presented/explored in the chosen poem with quotations and/or specific reference to support the answer.

   4-3 marks
   identify and comment on one or two aspects of the way strong emotions are presented/explored in the chosen poem with quotations and/or specific reference to support the answer.

   2-1 marks
   a generalised acknowledgement that there are strong emotions in the chosen poem, with some generalised reference to the text.

NATIONAL 5 ENGLISH
MODEL PAPER 3

Reading for Understanding, Analysis and Evaluation

1. Any two of the following:
   - the bluntness/brevity/content of the opening sentence
   - "hundreds of others" is emphasised by use of parenthesis
   - the use of the colon isolates or enforces the pause before "Soweto"
   - the positioning of "Soweto" gives a climactic effect.

2. Any three of the following for one mark each:
   - because of the law/rule enforcing/requiring use of Afrikaans in schools
   - because they saw this as offensive/demeaning
   - because this came on top of other examples of poor treatment
   - because loss of language means loss of free thought
   - because they were generally being downtrodden, denied freedom.

3. Any four of the following for one mark each:
   - he stood up to authority
   - although he was weak, he showed he was not afraid
   - his story illustrated that there is suffering/hardship everywhere
   - he gave inspiration to young black South Africans
   - they were amazed that the book/story had not been prohibited
   - his creator seemed to understand human suffering.

4. One mark for selection of word and one for comment. Any two of the following:
   - "frail" — suggests undernourished, etc
   - "courageous" — suggests he was willing to stand up for himself, etc
   - "oppression" — suggests he suffered severely at the hands of his masters
   - "slave labour" — suggests he was treated cruelly, unfairly, inhumanely, etc
   - "thin rations" — suggests the extreme meagreness of his food
   - "cruel" — suggests vindictive, spiteful nature of his enemies
   - "taunts" — suggests the malicious, aggressive behaviour of his enemies.

5. It introduces an explanation of the way in which they "took Oliver to heart".

6. Any four of the following for one mark each (may be in bullet point form or in prose):
   - his books were shared among many people
   - there was a waiting list for his books
   - he inspired the formation of a committee dedicated to improving conditions among young black people
   - his characters were known well, referred to by name
   - he connected people to the great books of the world
   - he was chosen as favourite by Hugh Masakela on *Desert Island Discs*.

7. Any two of the following for one mark each:
   - they were not interested in black people improving themselves
   - they were actively opposed to black people improving themselves
   - they were tyrannical, vicious, over-severe in punishment
   - they were ruthless
   - they were dishonest/corrupt (the charge of "violence" for a non-violent act.

8. (a) • (first) the idea of grandparents carrying out initial education then strongly encouraging as much learning as possible
   - (second) the idea of encouraging isolated/primitive peoples to understand/have control over their own world/environment
   - (third) the idea of using your own language to learn about your own world.

   (b) One mark for selection of word or feature and one mark for comment. Any two of the following:
   - "love" — shows books were treated with respect, passion, devotion, etc
   - "inspire" — suggests leading towards something uplifting, etc
   - "mentor" — idea of helpful, inspirational teacher
   - "spent a lifetime" — idea of dedication, devotion to a worthy cause
   - "future" — suggests hope, improvement, etc
   - short sentence "And they got it." — triumphant tone
   - "sacrifices" — suggests a worthwhile, if costly, course of action, done for the benefit of others
   - "applaud" — idea of approval, support, etc.

NATIONAL 5 ENGLISH MODEL PAPER 3

Critical Reading

SECTION 1 — Critical Essay

Please see the assessment criteria for the Critical Essay on pages 84 to 85.

SECTION 2 — Scottish Context

SCOTTISH TEXT (DRAMA)

Bold Girls by Rona Munro

1. A contrast clearly defined and suitable textual reference for two marks. Any of the following contrasts:
   - Cassie's extroversion versus Marie's shyness
   - Cassie's confidence versus Marie's timidity
   - Cassie's self-centredness versus Marie's obliging nature
   - Cassie's exuberance versus Marie's diffidence.

   Reference could be made to any of the following to support any of the contrasts:

   Words:
   - Marie: "Well, maybe …"
   - Marie: the rather feeble meat pie joke – attempted humour
   - Cassie "great diet"
   - Cassie: "really feel the benefit"
   - Cassie: "Let them".

   Actions:
   - Marie: *"shuffling cautiously"*
   - Marie: *"glances round nervously"*
   - Cassie: *"dancing … extravagant"*
   - Cassie: *"beams, applauding"*.

2. A valid aspect of the relationship and appropriate textual support for two marks. Possible answers include:
   - Marie cares for/is concerned about Cassie ("Cassie, what's wrong?", "Have you had words?")
   - Marie is supportive of Cassie ("It'll be all right Cassie.", "I'll just be across the road, I won't let you go crazy.")
   - Cassie feels she can confide in Marie ("I tell you Marie I can't stand the *smell* of him.")
   - Cassie knows Marie is unshockable, knows she can exaggerate with her ("I'm just bad, Marie, didn't you know?")
   - there is a kind of unspoken understanding between them (*"Slowly Cassie smiles at her."*).

3. A straightforward comment on a valid feature for one mark; two marks for a more extended comment. Possible answers include:
   - the use of italics to emphasise her disgust/contempt
   - "greasy" — suggests unhealthy, slimy, etc
   - "grinning" — suggests leering, unpleasant, etc

   - "beer bellied" — suggests self-indulgence, unpleasant, sloppy appearance
   - "winking away" — suggest lecherous, unsavoury, etc
   - "wriggling" — makes him sound worm-like
   - "fat fingers" — suggests clumsy, distasteful, etc
   - "like I'm a poke of chips" — he treats her as a commodity, something for his own gratification
   - alliteration ("greasy, grinning", "beer bellied", "fat fingers") — harsh sounds emphasise her revulsion
   - climactic structure of the last sentence — builds to the horror of "my *bed*".

4. Answers should focus on the relationship between Marie and Cassie and must take account of the revelations in Scene Four.

   Marks are allocated as follows:

   8-7 marks
   identify and comment on three or four aspects of the relationship between Marie and Cassie as demonstrated in the play with quotations and/or specific examples to support the answer.

   6-5 marks
   identify and comment on two or three aspects of the relationship between Marie and Cassie as demonstrated in the play with quotations and/or specific examples to support the answer.

   4-3 marks
   identify and comment on one or two aspects of the relationship between Marie and Cassie as demonstrated in the play with quotations and/or specific examples to support the answer.

   2-1 marks
   a generalised acknowledgement of the relationship between Marie and Cassie, with some generalised reference to the text.

SCOTTISH TEXT (PROSE)

The Testament of Gideon Mack by James Robertson

1. Any three of the following points for one mark each:
   - Gideon is watching TV (on a Sunday)
   - his father returns unexpectedly
   - his father is furious
   - his father forces him to watch rest of programme
   - his father delivers a condemnation of American culture.

2. Any two of the following possible answers for one mark each:
   - switches off the TV even though he knows there is no point
   - "jumped to my feet" — sudden action implying nervousness
   - "a flush of shame and fury" — embarrassment and resentment
   - futile action of trying to protect the TV set
   - "bowed my head" — can't look his father in the face
   - fixes eye on crack — trying to shut out the presence of his father
   - "mumbled" suggests he is confused, in a panic.

3. A straightforward comment with appropriate reference for one mark; two marks for a more extended comment. Possible answers include:

   - use of italics to convey tone of voice
   - rhetorical question to express fury at disobedience
   - hint of cutting sarcasm in "you have become very skilled at operating that thing"
   - "huge right hand descended on my neck" – sense of monstrous threat
   - "thumb and fingers gripped" – conveys the tightness, painfulness of the action
   - "increased the pressure" – making it even worse
   - "thought my head would snap off" – no thought for Gideon's pain
   - "breathing was like that of some monstrous creature in its den" – the comparison dehumanises his father, makes him sound like a mythical destroyer
   - "If I squirmed … his grip tightened" – no mercy, prepared to inflict even greater pain
   - "he pushed me" – forceful, aggressive action.

4. A straightforward comment with appropriate reference for one mark; two marks for a more extended comment; a fully developed single point will be awarded three marks.

   Possible answers include:

   - the way he says "What … is … that?" as if spitting out the words in disgust
   - his refusal to call the programme by it correct name, preferring "Bat … man" as if the words are disgusting
   - "whatever that means" – implying it might mean anything
   - "drivel" – he thinks it's worthless, idiotic
   - "unutterable garbage" – he considers it to be like rubbish, indescribably useless
   - "Garbage from the land of garbage." – repetition/ alliteration – harsh consonant conveys anger, disgust
   - "land of garbage" – implying whole country is contaminated.

5. Answers should show a good knowledge of the chosen incident and an ability to see its significance to the novel as a whole. Almost any incident in the novel could be used: "big ones" (such as the death of Jenny, the finding of the Stone, falling into the Black Jaws, his dialogue with the Devil, Miss Craigie's funeral) but also many smaller significant incidents throughout the novel.

   Marks are allocated as follows:

   8-7 marks
   explore effectively and in detail the chosen incident and its importance to the development of character, using quotations and/or specific reference to support the answer.

   6-5 marks
   explore in some detail the chosen incident and its importance to the development of character, using quotations and/or specific reference to support the answer.

   4-3 marks
   explore at a basic level the chosen incident and its importance to the development of character, using quotations and/or specific reference to support the answer.

2-1 marks
some knowledge of the chosen incident with only minimal reference to its importance in the development of character.

SCOTTISH TEXT (POETRY)

Poems by Jackie Kay

1. Possible answers include:

   - refers to the colour of the drink
   - it is something associated with childhood/happier times.

2. Any two of the following, not necessarily with textual support, for one mark each; or any one of the following with clear textual support:

   - negative: "they only wilt and die", "Don't bring …" (x2)
   - passive: "nods off", "fades"
   - dismissive: "Orange nostalgia, that's what that is"
   - tired of hospital experience: "whole day was a blur, a swarm of eyes"
   - distrusting: "Those doctors with their white lies."
   - scornful/cutting: "Did you think you could cheer me up with a *Woman's Own*?"

3. Possible answers include:

   - "grapes have no imagination, they're just green" – shows she has no interest in them, because they are featureless, dull, have nothing to appeal to her …

   whereas

   - "the big brandy, the generous gin, the Bloody Mary, the biscuit tin, the chocolate gingers, the dirty big meringue?' – seem livelier, more appealing because of their association with sharp taste, colour, excess, … (appropriate comment could be made also on the alliteration, the list structure and the self-indulgent glee of "dirty big meringue").

4. Answers should define clearly at least one mood and support it with valid close reference to the text of the poem. One mark for identification of acceptable mood(s), and one mark for each explanation from the text. Possible answers include:

   mood:

   - happy, upbeat, optimistic, positive, reassured, …

   references:

   - "clear her cupboard" – hint of a new start, getting rid of the unwanted
   - "bags full" – sense of a job well done
   - "wave with her flowers" – cheerful gesture
   - "My mother … waves back" – gesture is reciprocated, sense of connection
   - "face is light and radiant" – she can see brightness, almost angelic light
   - "sheets billow and whirl" – sense of freshness, unrestrained movement
   - "She is beautiful" – a straightforward statement of affection

- "the empty table is divine" — by clearing away all the unwanted things, she has made a simple table seem somehow holy
- "singing an old song" — implying contentedness and connection with her mother.

5. Answers should focus on a suitable poem and on the way a relationship between generations is presented and explored in it. Any of the poems on the set list would be suitable. It is acceptable in this question to write about a poem by Jackie Kay which is not on the set list.

Marks are allocated as follows:

8-7 marks
identify and comment on three or four aspects of the way the relationship between generations is presented/explored in the chosen poem with quotations and/or specific reference to support the answer.

6-5 marks
identify and comment on two or three aspects of the way the relationship between generations is presented/explored in the chosen poem with quotations and/or specific reference to support the answer.

4-3 marks
identify and comment on one or two aspects of the way the relationship between generations is presented/explored in the chosen poem with quotations and/or specific reference to support the answer.

2-1 marks
a generalised acknowledgement that the chosen poem explores a relationship between generations, with some generalised reference to the text.

SCOTTISH TEXT (POETRY)

Poems by Edwin Morgan

1. Two brief explanations for one mark each. Possible answers include:
   - "Christmas lights" — bright and cheerful, association with festivity, etc
   - "the three of them are laughing" — everyone is in a good mood
   - "a cloud of happiness" — even their breath is associated with joy
   - "Wait till he sees this but!" — sense of anticipation, pleasure in giving.

2. For each choice: a basic point for one mark and two marks for a more sophisticated comment. Possible answers include:

   the chihuahua:
   - cute, appealing, vulnerable ("tiny")
   - colourful, perhaps a little dignified ("Royal Stewart tartan")
   - a little ridiculous, incongruous ("coat like a teapot-holder").

   the baby:
   - clean, pure ("white shawl")
   - radiant, alert ("all bright eyes")
   - like a good luck charm ("mouth like favours")
   - sweet, appealing, nourishing ("in a fresh sweet cake").

   the guitar:
   - like something alive, organic ("swells out")
   - bright, associated with decoration and with giving ("silver tinsel tape")
   - associated with celebration, mystical powers ("brisk sprig of mistletoe").

3. Four simple points for one mark each, but some answers will provide a convincing response by dealing with fewer than four points. Possible answers include:
   - they are objects of wonder/admiration
   - they are a celebration of life
   - they render Christ's birth in a sense irrelevant
   - they have the power to defy death
   - they are united like a conquering army
   - they can overcome any threat.

4. An acceptable comment and textual reference for two marks. Possible answers include:
   - positive ("vanished … yet not vanished")
   - uplifted, inspired ("…they wind/the life of men…")
   - confident, safe ("laughter ringing them round like a guard")
   - saddened, depressed ("vanished … end … winter").

5. Answers should focus on a suitable poem and on how the poet "transforms the ordinary". Of the poems on the set list, the most profitable will be: "In the Snack-bar" or "Winter" or "Good Friday". It is acceptable in this question to write about a poem by Morgan which is not on the set list.

Marks are allocated as follows:

8-7 marks
explore effectively and in detail how the chosen poem transform the ordinary into something special and thought-provoking, using quotation and/or specific reference to support the answer.

6-5 marks
explore in some detail how the chosen poem transform the ordinary into something special and thought-provoking, using quotation and/or specific reference to support the answer.

4-3 marks
explore at a basic level how the chosen poem transform the ordinary into something special and thought-provoking, using quotation and/or specific reference to support the answer.

2-1 marks
some knowledge of the chosen poem with only minimal reference to the idea of transforming the ordinary.

Acknowledgements

Permission has been sought from all relevant copyright holders and Hodder Gibson is grateful for the use of the following:

An extract fom the article 'Reassuring Message of Rowling's Wizard World' taken from 'The Scotsman', June 2003 © The Scotsman Publications Ltd (SQP Reading for Understanding, Analysis and Evaluation pages 2 & 3);

An extract from 'The Steamie' copyright 1990 © Tony Roper. Excerpted with permission of Nick Hern Books Ltd: www.nickhernbooks.co.uk (SQP Critical Reading page 5);

An extract from 'Treasure Island' by Robert Louis Stevenson published by Cassell and Company Ltd 1883. Public domain (SQP Critical Reading pages 7 & 8);

The poem 'Song Composed in August' by Robert Burns, 1783. Public domain (SQP Critical Reading page 9);

The article 'Superstition' by Matthew Syed © The Times/NI Syndication, 1st July 2009 (Model Paper 1 Reading for Understanding, Analysis and Evaluation pages 2 & 3);

An extract from 'Sailmaker' by Alan Spence. Reproduced by permission of Hodder Education (Model Paper 1 Critical Reading pages 4 & 5);

An extract from 'The Cone Gatherers' by Robin Jenkins reprinted by permission of Peters Fraser & Dunlop (www.petersfraserdunlop.com) on behalf of the Estate of Robin Jenkins (Model Paper 1 Critical Reading pages 7 & 8);

An extract from the short story 'Away In A Manger', taken from 'Hieroglyphics and Other Stories' by Anne Donovan, published by Canongate Books (Model Paper 1 Critical Reading pages 9 & 10);

The poem 'Anne Hathaway' by Carol Anne Duffy, taken from 'The World's Wife', published by Picador 1999. Reproduced by permission of Pan Macmillan (Model Paper 1 Critical Reading page 11);

An extract from the article '2b or not 2b' by David Crystal from 'The Guardian' 5th June 2008. Originally from 'txtng: the gr8 db8' published by Oxford University Press, 2008 © David Crystal (Model Paper 2 Reading for Understanding, Analysis and Evaluation pages 2 & 3);

An extract from 'Tally's Blood' by Ann Marie di Mambro, published by Education Scotland. Reprinted by permission of Ann Marie di Mambro/MacFarlane Chard Associates (Model Paper 2 Critical Reading pages 4 to 6);

An extract from 'Kidnapped' by Robert Louis Stevenson, published by Cassell and Company Ltd 1886. Public domain (Model Paper 2 Critical Reading page 7 & 8);

An extract from the story 'In Church' by Iain Crichton Smith, taken from 'The Red Door', published by Birlinn. Reproduced by permission of Birlinn Ltd. www.birlinn.co.uk (Model Paper 2 Critical Reading page 9);

An extract from 'Visiting Hour' by Norman MacCaig, taken from 'Three Scottish Poets', published by Canongate Books. Reproduced by permission of Birlinn Ltd. www.birlinn.co.uk (Model Paper 2 Critical Reading pages 11 & 12);

An extract adapted from an article by Carol Lee in The Times 10th June 2006, from her book 'A Child Called Freedom' (Thistle e-book). (Model Paper 3 Reading for Understanding, Analysis and Evaluation pages 2 & 3);

Bold Girls copyright © 1991 Rona Munro. Excerpted with permission of Nick Hern Books Ltd: www.nickhernbooks.co.uk (Model Paper 3 Critical Reading pages 4 & 5);

An extract from 'The Testament of Gideon Mack' (Hamish Hamilton 2006, Penguin Books 2007). Copyright © James Robertson, 2006. Reproduced by permission of Penguin Books Ltd. (Model Paper 3 Critical Reading pages 7 & 8);

The poem 'Lucozade' by Jackie Kay, taken from 'Darling: New & Selected Poems' (Bloodaxe Books, 2007) (Model Paper 3 Critical Reading page 9);

The poem 'Trio' by Edwin Morgan, taken from 'New Selected Poems' published by Carcanet Press Limited, 2000 (Model Paper 3 Critical Reading page 11).

Hodder Gibson would like to thank SQA for use of any past exam questions that may have been used in model papers, whether amended or in original form.